A HISTORY OF
MILWAUKEE DRAG

A HISTORY OF
MILWAUKEE DRAG

Seven Generations of Glamour

MICHAIL TAKACH & B.J. DANIELS

Published by The History Press
Charleston, SC
www.historypress.com

Cover photo of B.J. Daniels by Ricky R. Heldt.

First published 2022

Manufactured in the United States

ISBN 9781467149174

Library of Congress Control Number: 2022933417

To Josie, to Jamie,
For teaching us all how to be seen.

CONTENTS

PREFACE

B.J. Daniels

When I was growing up in rural Wisconsin in the 1960s, LGBTQIA were just letters in the alphabet. Now, decades later, they signify community and my chosen family. Doing the research for this book, by combing through the thousands of clippings and photos I have collected from my drag career, I am overwhelmed with so many emotions. It's like when a room in an old house has been wallpapered countless times, and when you start stripping the layers away, the past is revealed.

From as far back as I can remember, I knew I was different, and it didn't really bother me or my parents for that matter. I watched the TV variety shows of the time with a keen eye to the female entertainers, especially what they wore and how they performed. Alone in my room, I would copy their moves and dream of feathers, sequins and glamour. I found ways to incorporate performing into my younger life by joining community theater, creating puppets, making their costumes and writing their shows.

By my teen years, I knew I was part of a movement that was sweeping the nation and the world, gay liberation. The discovery of gay bars in Madison when I was seventeen sealed the deal for me, and from then on, my goal was to become a star. Silly though that may sound, I pursued it with everything I had. I went out in drag as often as I could, and I loved the attention and praise I received for my "fishy look."

In 1980, I entered and won the very first Miss Gay Madison Pageant. I knew that it would help me enormously and used it as a springboard to make a career out of being a drag performer. Based on my picture in LGBT publications at the time, I was invited to join the *Who's No Lady Revue* by its director Samantha "Sam" Saglin and her star performer Ginger Spice in Milwaukee in 1981. Soon I found myself performing at Club 219 and other venues around town. It was a heady time for someone in their early twenties. Little did I know at the time that this city would become a sort of school of the creative arts for me and countless others over the next four decades.

Milwaukee's bar scene provided an environment for experimentation and escape, especially in the '80s, when so much was happening all at once. Drag was changing, morphing and becoming a centerpiece of gay life more than ever before. The AIDS crisis enveloped *all* of us, and an entertainer's job was also to advocate for LGBT causes. There is a sense of solidarity for those of us entertainers from that time who are still here to tell the tales of those who have gone before us. That is precisely what this book is about: to remember, reflect and celebrate the people and places that have led us to the writing of this important piece of history as it relates to the city of Milwaukee.

A History of Milwaukee Drag: Seven Generations of Glamour was pieced together by Michail and me with love and a commitment to honor the LGBTQIA performers of *all* kinds who have made the drag scene here the vibrant symbol of hope and defiance of societal norms it has always been and continues to be.

ACKNOWLEDGEMENTS

Without all the performers over all the generations, including those we could not personally mention or picture in our book, this book would not exist. While there are far too many to feature in these pages, we cannot overlook the building blocks they have created for the drag community simply by their fierce existence. We thank anyone, and everyone, who has summoned the courage to step onto the stage and be seen.

We are thankful for the relentless support and limitless resources of the Wisconsin LGBTQ History Project, Milwaukee County Historical Society, Milwaukee Public Library and UWM Archives.

INTRODUCTION

Michail Takach

"Want to come see my sister's show?"

October 1988 was one of the darkest months of my entire life. The school year had barely begun when my mother was killed in a shocking car accident. Less than a month later, a childhood friend died by suicide under still mysterious and somewhat haunting circumstances. Halloween was just around the corner, but for my newfound New Wave friends and me, every day was Halloween. Our hair was huge (and hugely flammable), our clothes were vintage (and extremely eccentric) and our music was angry, sinister and unsettling. Looking back, I was barely functional, but functional enough to avoid therapy, medication or being labeled "at-risk."

I met Melody a few weeks earlier, when my mother was still alive and I lived in a different timeline. She had just moved to our rural high school from points afar, and she wasn't really having this small-town experience. She'd drop me long and colorful notes, like telegrams from another world, with sordid stories about out-of-control house parties, amazing concerts, chaotic teenage romance and underage nightclubbing. She'd always invite me to tag along on these adventures.

And she'd always ask, over and over, "Want to come see my sister's show sometime?"

I would always think, "Sure, sometime."

Vanessa Alexander, circa 1988. *Melody Stephens.*

And then, one Saturday night, I was presented the choice of attending a hometown Halloween party or accepting Melody's longstanding invitation. And I remember her saying, "No more sometimes. Tonight, we're going!"

And so, we went. And that night expanded my world significantly.

I had no idea where I was going or what I was getting into. The bar, as it turned out, was in a murky neighborhood that added an edge of danger and excitement to our night out. We were quietly ushered upstairs through a side entrance and stumbled into an open-concept apartment filled with makeup mirrors, blow-dryers, dresses, wigs, makeup, cigarette smoke, music and bottles of booze. Nobody batted an eye at these obvious teenagers lurking around in their space.

When Vanessa saw us, she shrieked, "Hey hon, how do my tits look?" while proceeding to honk them like horns. I'll never forget what a fascinating force of nature she was that night; she talked a million miles an hour about everything and nothing, flitting around this mess of a room, while "putting on her face." Finally, she turned to us and said, "Look, you can stay for the show, but there are rules: do not change seats, do not talk to anyone and if the cops show up, run like hell!"

The next thing I knew, we were seated in the front row with two Blue Hawaiians we didn't order, didn't pay for and were being constantly refilled. As the curtain rose on Holly Brown & Company, I realized that Melody's sister was (what we would today call) a trans woman, performing alongside female impersonators, and I was at my very first drag show. Never once had Melody mentioned any of this in advance. And it wasn't that she was trying to deceive me: this *was* her sister's show, after all, and it was one hell of a show at that. Although I had gay and lesbian people in my family, and I knew gay bars existed, I had no idea they were anything quite like this. I'd seen drag shows on TV before, but they were nothing like this at all. This was an over-the-top cinematic experience so intense that I almost forgot I was in Milwaukee.

I was spellbound. And it wasn't just the Blue Hawaiians.

Holly Brown & Company was selling out three shows a week at the time, inviting crossover crowds so starved for edgy and original entertainment that they'd visit gay bars to get it. At the time, La Cage and Club 219 were locked in mortal combat to host Milwaukee's most glamorous drag productions—unlike anything the city had ever seen before, in terms of quality, talent, design, experience and reputation. The luster of these shows was so addictive that people would attend several shows a week to get their fix. The competition was so fierce that bar owners would forbid "their" performers and staff from visiting other venues. Rumor has it, some even paid their talent extra to stay out of the other bars. They were more than assets: the queens of that era were nothing less than Milwaukee royalty, commanding power not only in the club but also at fashion shows, art galleries, restaurant openings, extravagant galas, photo shoots and more. They enjoyed power and privilege unprecedented in local history.

It was truly a golden age of drag—and I had literally stumbled into the middle of it. Over the next few years, I spent far, far more time at La Cage's shows than I am willing to admit, alongside others my age who earned their own early access one way or another. Together, we found our community, and we found some light in that late '80s era known for its endless, inescapable darkness. Some of them would even find themselves on that stage later on.

Although I was strictly part of the audience, I knew there was something magical about my experience. From that very first night, I recognized there

Holly Brown & Company, photographed by Francis Ford in the late 1980s. *B.J. Daniels.*

was an energy crackling around that stage, an energy that was both magnetic and transformative, a sorcery of sorts that transformed both performer and performance into something bigger, something more exciting, something larger than life.

Little did I know that brave artists had been tapping into that magic in Milwaukee for generations. Little did I suspect that entertainers have harnessed the power of glamour to enchant, intoxicate and seduce their audiences since the 1880s. And little did I know that Indigenous people who transcended gender were revered as extraordinary beings in prehistoric times.

Before the European conquest of what would become Wisconsin, there were no known legal or social punishments for sexual or gender identity. Native American tribes had been recognizing and celebrating two-spirit people since ancient times. These revered individuals were supported throughout their lives: there was no "coming out" moment, they were recognized as neither male nor female but a third, alternative gender. Children would pursue their gender, as it came to them, at a young age. The Potawatomi, Winnebago and Ojibwe Nations gave the two-spirited elevated roles: doctors, peacemakers, mediators, matchmakers and name-givers. The Potawatomi called these people M'netokwe, meaning "supernatural" or "extraordinary," and they were highly respected in their society.

European explorers and Christian missionaries immediately saw the two-spirit as a challenge to their authority. They were a variation that challenged all the colonizers knew of gender. And over 150 precolonial Native American tribes fully supported the variation.

The two-spirit were perceived to be dangerous—even more dangerous than the tribal chiefs—as they were believed to hold supernatural powers. Tribal chiefs were often forced to surrender their two-spirit people to save the rest of their tribe. These promises were usually broken, as conquerors sought to dehumanize the Indigenous. Many two-spirit people were brutalized, tortured, subjected to "corrective rape" and murdered. Some were fed to dogs. Any survivors were incarcerated, forced to wear misgendered clothing and "reeducated" in Christian beliefs and government schools.

Throughout the 1850s, cities across the Upper Midwest (including Chicago and Milwaukee) introduced "masquerade laws" prohibiting cross-dressing. These laws were heavily—even brutally—enforced for one reason only: to keep that magic on lockdown.

Ever since, America has been in a viciously toxic love-hate relationship with female impersonators, alternately celebrating and applauding their craft while condemning and outlawing their existence. For generations, the magic they wield has inspired passion and panic like no other type of performance.

Yet somehow, Milwaukee—of all places—has been a gold mine of celebrity drag since the 1880s. How has small-town, blue-collar, modest-to-a-fault Milwaukee launched so many local queens, regional pageant winners and even international drag superstars, including four (and counting) *RuPaul's Drag Race* contestants?

By exploring seven generations of Milwaukee history, we can see this ongoing contradiction of fear versus fascination inspired increasingly visible queer communities and venues until alignment with an earlier-than-expected gay resistance movement finally brought drag—and the full spectrum of gender identities—explosively out into the open, with much more complexity, confidence and sophistication than other Midwest cities.

Today, drag may seem more mainstream than ever—safe for all ages through drag queen story hours, drag brunches and drag reality shows galore—but this acceptance is rooted in a long history and heritage in places like Milwaukee. In places like La Cage and Club 219. At shows like Holly Brown's and Ginger Spice's. Drag was here in the 1950s, when my grandparents saw the Jewel Box Revue at the Tic Toc Club. Drag was here in the 1930s, when the Chez Paree was serving up free champagne for wayward West Siders. Drag was here in the 1910s at the Orpheum theater, in the 1890s at the riverside amusement parks and in the Grand Opera Hall in City Hall Square in June 1884.

Drag has been in Milwaukee almost as long as there has been a Milwaukee. Throughout history, both definitions of the word *glamour* could fairly be applied: "an attractive, appealing or exciting quality" and "to cast a spell or enchantment upon an unsuspecting person." And that's exactly what people love and fear about it.

Sadly, the golden age of Milwaukee drag ended not with a thunderous roar but a terrifying silence. AIDS stole one generation of men from history and traumatized the generation that followed. So many stars of the stage so long ago departed, as well as so many audience members, that 1988 now feels like a century ago. Sometimes, it's agonizing to think of all the encores, reunions and reinventions that can never happen today.

In Milwaukee, yesterday's applause has long echoes. We choose not to cry because it's over but smile because it happened. So, please join us on this guided tour across seven generations of glamour, as we celebrate how these heroes changed our city forever—and continue to change it today.

1

THE BIRTH OF THE
PRIMA DONNA (1884–1912)

Minstrel shows were popular in Chicago throughout the 1860s and 1870s, including female impersonators Burt Shepherd and Burton Stanley, but Milwaukee was not yet large enough—or sophisticated enough—to attract traveling talent until the 1880s. In 1884, Milwaukee was still a gas-lit city of unpaved, unsanitary dirt roads, where crumbling settlers' cottages were quickly being replaced by the financial and commercial temples of a new German Athens. It was a city changing so fast—in a world changing fast—that nobody could quite be sure what the future held.

On June 7, 1884, Francis Leon performed what is believed to be the first "drag" show in Milwaukee history at Nunnemacher's Grand Opera House in City Hall Square. Born Francis Patrick Glassey on November 21, 1844, the artist was first billed as "The Famous Leon" long before he was ever famous.

Leon was known for his performance as a blackface opera diva—an art form especially popular by the American Civil War. He made his Chicago debut on July 18, 1860, to the delight of the *Chicago Tribune*. "Lovers of amusement can while away two pleasant hours and gain ten pounds of laughing flesh," wrote the critics.

In 1863, he joined Arlington and Donniker's Minstrels for a tour that opened at the Chicago Opera House and later toured the country. His wardrobe included over three hundred dresses, some of which cost as much as $400. Eventually, he became so famous that marquees billed him only as "Leon."

By 1884, Leon and Kelly were famous on three continents. *Wisconsin LGBTQ Histtory Project.*

"Leon is the best male female actor known to the stage. He does it with such dignity, modesty, and refinement that it is truly art," according to the *New York Clipper.* "He could make a fool of a man if he wasn't sure. Heaps of boys in my area don't believe it's a man."

In 1864, he opened a successful theater with his partner and lover, Edwin Kelly. They hosted relief concerts for Civil War widows and their families. The couple returned to New York in 1867 to open their own performance troupe.

Leon and Kelly experienced public harassment and discrimination because the petite, ninety-seven-pound Leon was considered "effeminate and womanly" even out of costume. It was okay for Leon to be feminine for other people's amusement; it was not okay, in Reconstruction America, to be gender nonconforming for one's own affirmation. An 1870 Chicago review exclaimed, "Leon is womanlier in his by-play and mannerisms than the most charming female imaginable."

By 1874, every minstrel company in the country had a Leon impostor, so Francis changed his stage name to "The Only Leon." Leon was the highest-paid American minstrel performer by 1880. The group toured almost

"He could make a fool of a man if he wasn't sure," said the *New York Clipper*. "And most in my area don't believe it's a man." *Wisconsin LGBTQ History Project.*

nonstop for fifteen years. In 1878, he and Kelly set sail for Australia, where Leon's drag act earned $11,000 a week.

Milwaukee was on their 1884 national tour, and the city could not have been more excited for it. Advertisements announced, "A New Departure in Minstrelsy, The Fun, The Singing, The Dancing, The Jokes, The Tumbling, are all combined in the Comedy Satire of Leon & Cushman and Burlesque of Ill-Fed-Dora. Leon and Cushman's minstrels—at the Grand—to-night. Leon is the finest female impersonator in the United States."

The *Milwaukee Sentinel* reflected after the show, "Mr. Francis Leon is cordially welcomed as a well-established favorite. The excellence of his female impersonations was amply attested during this first visit, to prevalent doubts and discussions as to whether the person rather vaguely described as 'the Only Leon' was really of the male or of the female sex."

In 1885, Leon and Kelly returned to Australia, where they operated the Nugget Theater. In 1890, they returned to Chicago to produce *Babes in the Wood*, with a budget-breaking cast of four hundred. Kelly and Leon split five years later after losing their fortune; Kelly failed to resurrect his career and died in 1899. Leon returned to Chicago, where he opened a Burlesque Opera Company that only lasted nine days.

And then the Only Leon seemed to disappear completely.

Only a few years after Leon's tantalizing performance, a strange story confounded Milwaukee even more. "Police Raid on a Dance House," read the widely reported January 15, 1887 headline, which colorfully described how the Washington police shut down a "drag" party of "invited black and white guests" in an elegant Fifth Street house. Two of the male dancers were naked. Five men, including Dorsey Swann, were arraigned as suspicious persons and presented at the station house in "silks, satins of bright colors, and feminine names."

Swann's national reputation preceded him. Born William Henry Younker in 1858, he was the first known person to identify as a "Queen of Drag" and the first known queer activist in American history. Formerly enslaved, he came to Washington, D.C., a free man in 1882. Sometime in the 1880s, Swann resurrected the old slave tradition of the cake walk—often exhibited or explained as "voguing"—as the central feature of an underground ballroom scene. Although secret invitations and ever-changing locations provided a level of discretion, the police somehow became aware of the House of Swann.

"Thirteen Black Men Surprised at Supper and Arrested," read an April 13, 1888 headline. The article further noted that "a big Negro named Dorsey was arrayed in a gorgeous dress of cream-colored satin" at Dorsey's thirtieth birthday party at a house at Twelfth and F. "The Queen stood in an attitude of royal defiance." While thirteen were arrested at the raid, an additional seventeen men—all in drag—escaped before the police arrived. It was noted that all were formerly enslaved. Dorsey blocked the police's entry and fought with officers so that partygoers could flee. The host, William Dorsey Swann, was quoted as saying, "You is no gentlemen" as the police shredded his gown during the arrest. The raucous arrest made quite a national impression, and over four hundred gathered to watch—and report—the raid.

"The Queen Raided: Unexpected Interruption to Her Banquet and Ball," read another headline. "Her Majesty Shows Fight with a Policeman—In the Contest Her Handsome Dress Torn Off."

Dorsey's birthday party raid was historically significant: it was the first arrest specifically for female impersonation in American history, the first time queer people fought back against police oppression and the first use of "queen" in print to describe a gender nonconforming person. National newspapers spoke about not only "drag balls" but also the concept of "drag" for the very first time. Milwaukee was nowhere near ready for this subculture. The idea that Black men, former slaves, were secretly gathering—in women's clothing—was confusing and terrifying. And the story wasn't over yet.

"A 'Drag Party' Raided," read a January 1, 1896 news story, as Washington police raided a quiet-looking house to find twelve men and one woman "attired in handsome silks and satins, each in complete feminine costume." Men were seen dancing together "in a nearly nude condition." Swann and three Black men were arrested, while the white men were let go. Nearly all the "girls" were bailed out, but "William Dorsey, who by the way, was the 'Queen,' was charged as being a suspicious character."

Swann was sentenced to three hundred days in jail for the false charge of "keeping a disorderly house"—otherwise known as a brothel—although there was no evidence of sex work. Newspaper reports spoke of him operating a "hell of iniquity," where young men of respectable parentage were seduced into a sordid life. Articles offered "fearful revelations of the downfall and ruin of Washington's youngest men."

"I would like to send you where you would never again see a man's face," said Judge Miller, "and I would like then to rid the city of all other disreputable people of your kind."

Published psychiatrists were no kinder. Dr. Charles Hamilton considered Swann a "victim of sexual inversion" and diagnosed ball-goers as "an organization of colored erotopaths" and "a lecherous group of sexual perverts." Dr. Irving Rose called them "a band of Negro men with androgynous characteristics."

Swann bravely appealed to President Grover Cleveland for a pardon, citing his community's right to organize without threat of violence. The pardon was denied on July 29, 1896. After serving out his sentence, Swann retired from hosting balls entirely. His younger brother Daniel Swann continued the House of Swann tradition until he died in 1954.

William Dorsey Swann died in Hancock, Maryland in 1925. After he died, local police burned down his house. No known photographs of him exist. Although multiple websites show images claiming to be him, these photos depict 1903 vaudeville performers.

Although "drags" continued in underground popularity in eastern cities through the 1920s, particularly New York City, there's no evidence that any significant ballroom culture existed in Milwaukee. But Swann was not the only one scandalizing Milwaukee with faraway tales of big-city vice.

In November 1878, national news broke about "Mrs. Noonan," a man who lived as a woman for at least a decade and married another man. Her husband, who had no idea he had married a "man," eventually committed suicide. As female impersonator shows came into minstrel vogue, the moral parable of Mrs. Noonan was firmly on midwestern minds.

On August 8, 1888, the Chicago news desk reported a police raid at 140 West Monroe Street in which one man was arrested in women's clothing and "servicing" the other three men. He claimed to be a famous female impersonator and was so feminine that he was nearly jailed with female prisoners. The story sparked significant concern in Chicago, Milwaukee and other Midwest cities that female impersonators were using their wiles offstage for "pervert practices."

In November 1892, two female impersonators were arrested at Mandel Brothers department store in Chicago for shoplifting women's gloves, silk stockings and undergarments, which they could not have legally purchased had they tried. It was illegal for unaccompanied men to purchase these items at the time. The story was widely reported across the United States.

The Chicago World's Fair featured several female impersonators whose acts were widely celebrated. Fatima, the most notorious of them all, danced with such "wild abandon" that police closed her show on morality clauses. She was considered a true threat to young male visitors—although she was, in fact, a biological male. (The Chicago police would later harass "exotic" female impersonators in the Slums of Cairo exhibit at the Century of Progress, as well as biological female Sally Rand, in 1933.)

In 1902, the *Chicago Tribune* visited a rooftop garden at 144 North Kedzie Avenue to find Francis Leon living in quiet obscurity. "Chicago Man Satisfied on a Roof: Home of Leon, Once Famous Female Impersonator," read the headline. Leon was quoted in the article:

> *I have nothing to regret, nothing to look forward to, nothing to do but enjoy my plants, my flowers and my birds. Perhaps I am lazy—but I want nothing better than to enjoy the luxuries of my garden. I have had enough activity. I worked hard for thirty years, and this is my reward, and it is great enough to satisfy me. I go about little, and I am contented to live here just as you see me. I still cherish memories of the stage as you will observe.*

He continued,

> *These are the remains of my costumes and the manuscripts of plays in which I figured. I should not want to part with any of them although I never expect to use them again. They are just interesting as keepsakes….I always went on the theory that the public wanted the best, and I never failed to give them the best. What is more, I never wore stage jewelry. My jewelry was always the real thing.*

Francis Leon died in August 1922. He is buried in Mount Carmel Cemetery in Hillside, Illinois.

THE FEMALE IMPERSONATOR AS FREAK

Before Leon's visit, female impersonators could be seen only at Milwaukee's Dime Museum, a cabinet of curiosities operated by Kohl & Middleton. The rotating collection included electric ladies, strongmen, twenty-toed babies, five-hundred-pound women, snake charmers, leopard-spotted men, people with albinism, "Aztec" warriors, living dolls, frog children, ventriloquists, dog tamers, jubilee singers, African lion slayers, tattooed women, men with ten-foot beards, dancing cockatoos, mummified Sioux warriors and Texas giants. The Dime Museum leveraged its excellent location, "across from the Plankinton House," to lure tourists and locals alike into its mysterious menagerie.

Above: Milwaukee's dime museums showcased genetic—and gender—curiosities. *Milwaukee Public Library.*

Right: Annie Hindle was known as "The Great Hindle, pet of the ladies." *Wisconsin LGBTQ History Project.*

ANNIE HINDLE

The Dime Museum often welcomed guests from the P.T. Barnum Circus, including the "Fiji Cannibals," the Sinhalese Family, Indian Princess Ne-Ne-Tah and Madagascar Princess Aggie. While wildly popular, the Dime Museum's agenda of exploitation sometimes went a little too far. The *Milwaukee Journal* commented, "The Dime Museum can make bushels more money if its manager will secure the next mayor and exhibit him as a freak. It would prove more an attraction than the Fiji Mermaid."

On August 25, 1884, the Dime Museum reopened under the management of Jacob Litt, who sought to rise above the shock and gore tactics to create a "family resort in the city." His upgraded program included Frank LeRoy, the celebrated female impersonator, and the first of many female impersonators to work at Litt's by 1888. LeRoy seems to have launched his career touring Midwest dime museums and ten-cent circuses before joining the vaudeville scene. He was still performing as late as 1908.

In Leon's wake, the Dime Museum exploited local interest in gender transformation. In November 1884, the Dime Museum welcomed Annie Hindle, the first internationally famous drag king. "Hindle, the male impersonator, has become a favorite. Her make-up as a dude is very good," said the *Milwaukee Journal*. Hindle went on to scandalize America by presenting as "Charles Hindle" and marrying two women after her husband died.

"Once she was a bride, and twice she has been a groom," said the *Chicago Tribune*. "Once she had a husband, and twice she had a wife, once she was a widow, once a widower, and now she is a husband again." The illusion was shattered. These controversies affected faith in her stage act; many began to speculate she had always been a genetic man, and her popularity quickly waned.

Although at its heart an exploitative freakshow, Jacob Litt's Dime Museum was remarkably inclusive and launched several lucrative careers for its otherwise marginalized stars.

After a June 9, 1885 fire, the Dime Museum closed for repairs. Litt's Mammoth Dime Museum reopened on August 25, 1885, with a new vaudeville company and hourly stage performances. In 1897, Jacob Litt left Milwaukee for New York. On September 27, 1905, he died of a stroke at age forty-six, leaving an estate exceeding $1.25 million.

GREAT LALA COOLAH, THE "Man Venus," became one of the biggest stars at the nearby Star Museum (735 North Plankinton Avenue). "The Half Man, Half Woman" was first billed in March 1897 at the Columbia Theater

COLUMBIA MUSEE
AND THEATER.
182–184 Third St.— O. L. Meister. Mg.
Hourly Stage Shows; 1 to 6, and 7 to 10 P. M.
COMMENCING SUNDAY MATINEE
LALA COOLAH
Half Man, Half Woman

The Great Lala Coolah was likely intersex and not an "impersonator" at all. *Milwaukee Public Library.*

before taking residency at the Star in 1898. "Behold the most wondrous of all monstrosities," read the advertisement, "the power[ful] form of a man combined with the delicate beauty of a woman. Is it he, she or it?"

Onstage, the Great Lala was a national sensation who toured the nation for three decades and eventually opened a dime museum of his own; offstage, he was Frank Fuller (1870–1931), who claimed to be a natural-born female who was discovered to have male genitals at age twelve. After marrying and divorcing a man, the Great Lala began living as a man. She was featured on the cover of the *History of Living Wonders*, a dime museum souvenir book published in 1916. Eventually, he became the star clown of the Barnum & Bailey Traveling Circus.

Frank Fuller died on July 8, 1931, in New Haven, Connecticut. He was credited, at the time, as the originator of the "he/she carnival act." Newspapers did not share that Fuller was most likely an intersex person, not the "female impersonator" he was so frequently billed as.

On March 18, 1932, Tod Browning's *Freaks* opened at the Palace Theater (535 West Wisconsin Avenue) with a marquee asking, "What Sex Is the Half-Man, Half-Woman?" and a character modeled after the Great Lala Coolah. The dime museums were just a strange, fleeting memory.

FEMALE IMPERSONATION AS VICE

On August 2, 1888, Herbert Crowley, a "celebrated female impersonator from Ries' South Side concert hall," was arrested for being drunk and disorderly offstage in women's clothing. He spent the night in jail until he agreed not to do this again.

Crowley later joined the Henry Burlesque Company, where he headlined "a dozen equally well-known first-rate female impersonators" at the People's Theater (Plankinton and Wisconsin) next door to the Star Museum. With a soprano voice as flawless as his makeup, Crowley was the company's breakout star, alongside novelties like the Forty Thieves Burlesque Company, "real" Spanish swordfighters, human contortionists, the Norse Giant and Lilly Clay's Living Pictures.

"It was the unanimous opinion, however, that Herbert Crowley, the female impersonator, was one calculated to deceive even an expert, and it is pretty hard to make a casual observer and listener believe that he is not in the presence of an attractive young woman," said the *St. Paul Daily Globe*. (Before his death in 1932, Crowley achieved national fame on the Orpheum vaudeville circuit with his *Six Sailors* show, which transformed six hunky World War I veterans into gorgeous women. To the end, audiences complimented how convincing he was as a woman, to the common conclusion that he had never been a man.)

With female impersonators exploding in popularity, social reformers became concerned about the mental health of America's cities. In 1889, Dr Frank Lydston reported a "colony of male sexual perverts in Chicago and in every community of size. They operate in accordance with definite and concerted plan in quest of subjects to gratify their abnormal sexual impulses. Often, they are characterized by effeminacy of voice, dress, and manner." A subsequent survey claimed sexual inversion was widespread in the United States with New York, Boston, Philadelphia, Washington, Chicago, St. Louis, New Orleans, San Francisco and Milwaukee as the "homosexual capitals."

Lydston was likely sensationalizing the "fairy" movement of his time, when young male prostitutes wore wigs, lipsticks, jewelry and telltale red neckties to sell oral sex on the seamier sides of town. Although their numbers were very small in Milwaukee, the fairies were a horror story to urban reformers of the era. Orphans were recruited and organized into live-work prostitution "cribs," often without heat or running water, and engaged in ongoing sex work unthinkable today. It was the worst possible fate imaginable—and at the same time, one of the best chances of survival for abandoned or orphaned children.

"Chicago has not developed a euphemism yet for these male perverts," wrote Dr. James G. Kiernan. "Yet we know they are here."

In Milwaukee, the fairy boys were found in the "Bad Lands" of the Fourth Ward, which extended west and north from Third and Wells to encompass most of the lower West Side between 1890 and 1920. A rare Milwaukee Police Department report from February 1, 1890, recognized the deviance afoot:

The saloon kept by Robert Thorpe…is a boarding-house for fairies, and a number of them constantly kept in this place.…The saloon at 231 West Water St known as the "Mad House" is one of the worst dives in the city, a resort for young prostitutes, thugs and thieves.…[A] saloon on the southwest corner of Wells and West Water is the most disreputable place in the city, patronized by the lowest element of deviance.…Your attention is especially called to the saloon kept by Phil Nolde…principally patronized by young boys and girls of a tender age, who spend their nights there in drunken orgies and other lewd conduct with criminals. This place has become such a nuisance that citizens are praying for its suppression.

Milwaukee did not have anything like Chicago's First Ward and South Side masquerade balls, which enabled queer people to "come out" for one night only and openly explore gender and sexual options. As a tavern town first and foremost, Milwaukee instead seemed to have a tavern for every walk of life, no matter how extreme their appetite.

Unaffectionately named by police officers around 1892, the Bad Lands were considered the most dangerous beat assignment in the city. Newspapers adopted the name and reported "Trouble in the Bad Lands" on a regular basis. The name invoked Gilded Age paranoia about primitive savages threatening modern society from the frontier and blatant racism about the rapidly growing African American community.

THE CURIOUS CASE OF FRANK BLUNT

On November 16, 1893, Frank Blunt was tried in Milwaukee for larceny. It was charged that Blunt stole $175 from J.G. Perkins while visiting his home in Fond du Lac. Blunt had claimed he was a long-lost nephew of Perkins and stayed with the family for several days. After Blunt left town, the money was discovered missing from a trunk and an empty wallet concealed in the chimney.

Larceny was the least interesting part of this trial. It was discovered that the prisoner was a long-missing woman, twenty-eight-year-old Annie Morris, who had been "living as a man" for the past fifteen years. She was born in Halifax, Nova Scotia, in 1865 and ran away at age thirteen due to her father's cruelties. She attached herself to a horse trader, Jesse Blunt, and passed as his son as they traveled across the country. Only Jesse Blunt knew the secret.

The story of Frank Blunt spread across the region and country. "Girl Posed as a Man—For Fifteen Years, a Man!" said newspaper headlines. "The arrest of Frank Blunt has brought to light what might be the foundation for a novel," said the *Milwaukee Journal* on July 13, 1893. Citizens were shocked to learn that, as Frank Blunt, a woman had been voting in Fourth Ward elections for several years.

The renamed Frank Blunt worked men's jobs, gambled in men's pool halls and even caroused with women in public. At one time, Frank even managed a Northwoods Wisconsin lumber camp: swamping, driving logs, teaming and cooking.

From 1886 to 1890, the Blunts operated a saloon on Reed Street (now 194 South Second Street) in Walker's Point. Jesse Blunt later operated a rooming house and retail coal business at 748 North Third Street in Milwaukee.

Frank Blunt became a popular figure in the Bad Lands of the Fourth Ward and somewhat of a gigolo, whose lavish lifestyle was funded by his female suitors.

"So many curious women called to see Frank Blunt at the Fond du Lac jail that he, she or it protested, and the sheriff now denies admission to see the girl-boy," said the *Milwaukee Journal* on July 20, 1893.

During the trial, a Milwaukee saloonkeeper confessed to nearly shooting Blunt dead for "paying heavy attention to his wife." "She always dressed stylishly, mingled with men, and succeeded in having an easy time of it," he told the court. "She was always very sporty in the city." Another

The former Blunt saloon at 194 South Second Street over a century later. *Wisconsin LGBTQ History Project.*

saloon owner reported that Blunt had taken off with his wife and $450 of the saloon's dollars. The saloonkeeper followed the couple to Chicago, Oshkosh and back to Milwaukee, but Blunt was "too cute to catch."

A court reporter noted that "at 5 foot 3, 147 pounds, she would present a sorry figure in women's clothes if she were told to put them on. Unrestrained by the lacing and the tight-fitting garments of her sex, her figure has developed so much more masculine than feminine in appearance."

Furthermore, it was discovered that Frank Blunt had married a wheat buyer's daughter, Lulu Seitz, in Fond du Lac. After six years, Frank began to run around with other women, and Lulu called for a divorce. Neither she nor her family ever knew Blunt was not a man. Later, Blunt married Gertrude Field of Eau Claire but had already separated from her at the time of the trial. For some reason, Field furnished all the money for Blunt's defense but could not afford bail. Field told the *Milwaukee Journal* she would fight the charges all the way to the Supreme Court.

The judge asked Frank Blunt why Annie Morris had chosen to live life as a man. Was this the only crime she had committed under a false identity? Frank told the judge that once he put on a man's suit, he felt like he was himself for the first time. He drank, smoked, swore and gambled as much as any roughneck, and this is who he felt himself to be: a man. He did not intend to return to women's clothing or a women's life, no matter what the verdict was.

Blunt was sentenced to one year in the state penitentiary by Judge Gilson in January 1894. "Wisconsin's Pantaloon Maiden Must Suffer," screamed the news headlines. Blunt's pride—and his refusal to be ridiculed—struck a nerve with the press. Frank Blunt was released early for good behavior on December 6, 1894, under the enforced identity of "Francis Morris." Frank Blunt was never heard from again, and he has largely been forgotten as the LGBTQ pioneer he was.

THE HOUSE OF MISS KITTY

While the police were focused on misbehaving Black men in the Bad Lands, they casually overlooked the wide-open red-light district flourishing at the riverfront. Known to "sporting men" nationwide, River Street was one of the city's most popular tourist attractions. Houses of ill fame were known in Milwaukee as early as the 1850s. Although the city outlawed prostitution in 1879, officials estimated ninety-five brothels were operating in Milwaukee by the mid-1880s. By 1910, over two hundred "resorts" flourished in the "tenderloin"—offering unspeakable sexual adventures any hour, any day. Recognizing that prostitution was now a $5 million local industry, Police Chief John Janssen and Mayor David Rose quietly allowed the Bad Lands to continue, neither officially encouraged nor discouraged.

One of the most famous proprietors was Katy Miller, aka Madame Kitty Williams (1864–1943). Her opulent forty-two-room bordello sat just outside the Bad Lands at 219 East State Street, a mere block from City Hall, to which tunnels were rumored to exist. While there are no known photos of Miss Kitty or the interior of her brothel, sporting guides describe the property (and services available) with tremendous detail. According to rumor, Miss Kitty was the only madam who employed gay men and female impersonators among her harem—offering truly taboo trade for high-ticket customers with discerning and discreet tastes. Miss Kitty grew up in San Francisco and spent some time in Chicago, and male prostitutes were not entirely unknown in either city of men.

In its famous 1911 report on prostitution and other illicit activities, *The Social Evil in Chicago*, the Chicago Vice Commission described a homosexual subculture of "at least 20,000." Milwaukee reformers never dared to put a number on paper.

Milwaukee's growing socialist movement saw River Street—and the greater Bad Lands—as a terrible and disgraceful embarrassment. The city vowed to replace the red-light district with respectable businesses. After Emil Seidel was elected Milwaukee's first socialist mayor—the first socialist mayor of any U.S. city—in 1910, River Street and the Bad Lands were doomed.

Miss Kitty's, the most salacious of all, was specifically targeted as the first to be shut down in 1911. By June 15, 1912, River Street had "the silence of a graveyard," as owners removed names and numbers from the abandoned houses.

But these efforts failed: a 1914 vice investigation found that not only were brothels still operating in the Bad Lands, but they were now to be found in all corners of the city as well. Once confined in a segregated district, prostitution had gone citywide. Kitty Williams testified that reformers had created an unemployment crisis by putting one thousand women with few other options for legal, gainful employment out of work.

By 1922, the Bad Lands had become a fading memory. "The change has been rapid," said the *Milwaukee Sentinel* on February 12, 1922. "Ten

Miss Kitty's house, the most majestic of all Milwaukee bordellos, long past its prime. *Wisconsin LGBTQ History Project.*

years ago, Milwaukee was a wide-open town, with its 'districts' right in the heart of the city. Then the lid was clamped down and the watchfulness of the authorities soon dispersed the habitues. The 'Bad Lands' have become business districts, and each year sees new buildings replacing the old shacks of years gone by. Night life is no longer confined to the underworld. The times have completely reversed themselves."

As the story goes, Miss Kitty became a bit of a fairy godmother to wayward gay youth in her golden years, opening her storybook home to those who had none. As strange as it now seems, Milwaukee's most notorious bordello became a notorious gay boardinghouse in its old age.

In 1939, she lost her tavern license under charges of "allowing the unsavory to congregate and conspire." Attempts to reopen failed, as the Common Council associated Kitty with "men of questionable moral character."

Kitty died in January 1943 at age seventy-nine after a long illness. Her estate (valued at about $469,000 in today's dollars) was divided among nieces and nephews, but no one would claim the notorious house. It sat crumbling at Water and State for twenty years until finally demolished in 1963. Red Arrow Park's ice rink sits on the footprint of this lost LGBTQ landmark.

MILWAUKEE'S FIRST MASQUERADE PANIC

Vaudeville created some of the first stars of the American stage and screen, among them, the nation's first famous female impersonators.

On June 22, 1895, the American Comic Opera company was held over for a third sold-out week at Schlitz Park's Wonderland Pavilion (near today's Eighth and Walnut). The "bill of unusual merit" included the "ingenue of all female impersonators," Lincoln Elwood. "The Great Elwood" enjoyed a long career on the Milwaukee vaudeville circuit, spending summers at the riverside and lakefront resorts and winters at the downtown theaters. He made a big name for himself at the brand-new Alhambra Theater (334 West Wisconsin Avenue) throughout the 1896 season.

"The weather was a bit cool at the popular Chute the Chutes resort," wrote the *Milwaukee Journal* on September 20, 1897, "but Elwood is still decidedly in the ring. Crowds are tremendous." Weekend shows ran from noon until midnight and promised six stunning costume changes per performance. The Great Elwood was invited back to headline Chute the Chutes for summer 1898. Sadly, it was the park's final season, and the chutes were dismantled and sold at auction in September 1898. The Great Elwood vanished, never to be heard of again.

By 1897, the reigning Alhambra queen was "Stuart," whose performance as Queen Isabella in *1492* received regional attention. "A better bill is rarely ever presented at any variety theater than the one which is daily confronting the footlights at the Alhambra this week. What can be more wonderful than Stuart the female impersonator? He stands high in the ranks of the profession," said the *Milwaukee Sentinel*.

Female impersonators were an unusual headliner at turn-of-the-century family fun parks. *Milwaukee Public Library.*

MANY OF OUR GENDER nonconforming ancestors are known to us not because they headlined a stage but because they were convicted of the crime of being themselves.

Millie Brown found out the hard way on August 29, 1899. Arrested on charges of "acting queer" outside the Alhambra Theater, Brown (aka Harry Hynes) appeared before a curious police court the next morning.

"It was a very queer mixture. The man has some very feminine ways," wrote the *Milwaukee Journal*. "He was clad in female attire with the exception of the wig. He held a handkerchief just as a girl does; he smoothed down her skirt like a girl; and when walking, held it up just like a girl does. He carried a purse and wore a straw hat trimmed with ribbons. But the features were masculine and unattractive. The hands were large and brawny, the gait was masculine and there was a fuzz of whiskers on the face. The fact the boy neglected to shave yesterday is what led to the arrest."

HARRY HYNES DISGUISED AS MILLIE BROWN

Millie Brown was accused of being part of a cross-dressing crime ring. *Wisconsin LGBTQ History Project.*

Hynes was pressured to confess there was no "Millie Brown." He stated that he had been unable to find work as a man for two years, so he was now living his life as a woman. After living in Edgerton, Wisconsin, for a while, he was now employed as a maidservant at a house on Eighth and St. Paul. His employer knew him only as a woman, and he begged the police not to reveal his true sex.

Witnesses revealed that Hynes was one of several vaudeville performers rumored to be "masquerading" as real women in everyday life. The police suspected that they were planning an organized crime spree, using the female gender as a disguise—although there was no evidence or basis for this accusation, and Hynes had no previous criminal record. Newspapers kept the panic alive by sharing hints and rumors of cross-dressing thieves spotted around Milwaukee.

When asked about his "sisters in crime," Hynes confided that he socialized with at least one other man "disguising" as a woman. Hynes threatened to smash the camera and lick the police when they tried to photograph him. "You fellows are making a monkey of me," he shouted angrily, "and I won't stand for it."

Harry Hynes was sentenced to sixty days at the House of Correction for masquerading as a woman. Neither he nor Millie Brown was ever heard from again, and no underground cross-dressing crime ring was ever proven to exist. The panic subsided, but the skepticism remained—and other female impersonators paid a high price for presenting as themselves.

ON OCTOBER 19, 1904, the *Milwaukee Journal* reported that "Miss Jackson," who drunkenly declared herself a member of one of the first families of Virginia, "scandalized residents of Silver City" by hiking up her skirts and exposing herself on National Avenue.

"Her voice was husky, but her attire was gorgeous. Her skirt was red and there was a soft frou-frou that spoke of silken garments. Her jacket was elaborate in the extreme, and her picture hat was laced with a gorgeous assemblage of tropical plumage." Upon closer inspection, it was discovered that Miss Jackson was an African American man. Miss Jackson was apprehended by Constable Cheesman of West Allis, who charged her with vagrancy.

In April 1910, La Nier Watts, known as "Trixie Watts," was wanted in Milwaukee for breaking into the Avon Hotel (444 North Cass Street) and stealing women's clothing for his stage shows. When asked what motivated the crime, La Nier said "womanly vanity." The judge, unimpressed, sent Watts to jail for a year.

Wisconsin legislators, in the spirit of reform, felt compelled to do something about the deviance in their midst. In August 1913, the state passed the Hoyt Bill, which authorized the sterilization of certain criminals, including the "mentally defective" and "sexually deviant." Homosexuals and gender nonconforming people were not safe from these diagnoses. Any method of sterilization that was deemed "safe and effective" was allowable.

However, the State Medical Board seemed conflicted about the use of these powers. From 1913 to 1932, fewer than four people were sterilized each year.

2

THE ROARING TWENTIES AND THE PANSY CRAZE (1913–1936)

With the Hoyt Bill, Wisconsin sent a chilling message of intolerance to the queer community. Fortunately, the elevation of the national vaudeville circuit created a new safe haven for gay men, lesbians and the gender nonconforming. Milwaukee became fascinated with the bigger-than-life personalities of visiting vaudeville celebrities, and an early community began to form within the performing arts.

QUEER AS A TWO-DOLLAR BILL: BURT SAVOY

One of the most famous female impersonators was Bert Savoy (1888–1923), originally of the Ziegfeld Follies and later the Greenwich Village Follies.

Savoy was born Everett McKenzie in Boston in 1876. He started his stage career as the understudy of a combination "cooch dancer" fortuneteller. He appeared in Miss 1917, Ziegfeld Follies of 1918, Hitchy-Koo, Cinderella on Broadway and the extremely gay-friendly Greenwich Village Follies of 1920 and 1922.

There was no pretense for Burt Savoy's drag: he simply dressed as a woman; behaved like a catty, loud and flamboyant woman; and delivered swishy, campy, leering comedy against straight man Jay Brennan. His comedy was openly gay in theme and content. He was the first female impersonator widely known as a queer man, and there were no public relations efforts to control him, change him or "straighten him up."

Savoy regularly employed feminine pronouns when referring to himself and a cadre of like-minded friends. Unlike other professional female impersonators of the day, he remained in costume and in character offstage. He was arrested more than once for cross-dressing offstage.

Savoy made his Milwaukee debut at the Davidson Theater (621 North Third Street) on January 22, 1922. His competition was Helen Keller performing with Anne Sullivan at the other end of the block at the Majestic Theater.

"Direct from the Garrick Theater Chicago, all of last season the toast of Manhattan's elite: The Gayest, Smartest and Most Highly Amusing of All the Girl-and-Music Shows," said the *Milwaukee Journal*. The *Milwaukee Sentinel* was not so kind: "Naturally, this being the genius revue, there is no attempt at anything in the way of a story, and the evening is therefore made up of a string of clever specialties....Savoy is the funniest of female impersonators, wearing the latest and most gorgeous of gowns, and firing off his funny lines in a hoarse voice that is a killing contest. Occasionally, the humor becomes a bit wild." Still, the show ran for three full weeks and became the biggest-grossing Davidson Theater show of 1922.

Savoy would only return to Milwaukee one more time. "Bert Savoy, in his funny travesty of the female impersonator, is wearing gorgeous gowns and telling amazing stories at the Orpheum," reported the *Milwaukee Sentinel* on June 10, 1923.

Only two weeks later, Burt Savoy's career ended as dramatically as it began. After a loud clap of thunder on a Long Island beach, Savoy was reported to say, "That'll be enough out of you, Miss God!" Savoy and his traveling companion Jack Grossman were struck dead by a bolt of lightning. For years, rumors circulated that he had an "unlucky two-dollar bill" in his pocket.

By November 1923, there were Burt Savoy impersonators. Many of his common sayings became part of drag vernacular. Incredibly, some of these (e.g., "you slay me") are still popular today. Many felt that Mae West appropriated Savoy's style, comedy and timing into her own character.

THE MAGIC OF JULIAN ELTINGE

Julian Eltinge (1881–1941) overcame a mundane childhood to become the highest-paid and most widely respected vaudeville actor in the world. Born William Julian Dalton in Massachusetts, the young Eltinge was sent to live

Julian Eltinge was long considered the master of female impersonation. *Wisconsin LGBTQ History Project.*

with an aunt in Boston, where he pursued stage training. The *Milwaukee Journal* first mentioned "J.T. Eltinge" on June 1, 1901, printing a photo of this popular burlesque actor amusing "Boston's exclusive set."

Unlike female impersonators before him, Eltinge sought to convince audiences he was a real woman. He toured the country under one name— "Eltinge"—while singing, dancing and performing in female roles. At the end of the show, he'd remove his wig, leaving the audience applauding for more. Entire shows were built around Eltinge as the single character, often with weak plots that allowed Eltinge to "display his versatility and femininity at its best."

Although Eltinge was almost certainly a closeted gay man, he was never widely suspected to be homosexual. He was masterful at separating his onstage feminine persona from his offstage masculine persona. As a man, Eltinge smoked cigars, boasted of hunting and fishing hobbies and even staged boxing matches to show off how "rugged" he was. He was known to attack stage workers, audience hecklers and reporters who speculated on his sexuality. When his career waned in 1927, he told the press that he was focused on operating a men's fitness resort in San Diego. When newspapers reported his July 1929 car crash, Eltinge was described as a fearless daredevil. In October 1931, he proudly publicized his war wounds after a battle with a 190-pound swordfish. He famously told a reporter, "I'm not gay, I just like pearls!"

As a woman, he was glamorous, delicate and alluring. Women went wild for Eltinge, while men found his success fascinating. Dorothy Parker referred to him as "ambisextrous," although there's never been any confirmation of him ever having a lover.

Eltinge's branding was decades ahead of its time. He was a twenty-year spokesperson for Nemo self-reducing corsets. He produced his own magazine, his own line of cigars for male fans and his own line of cosmetics for female fans. He built a Spanish Colonial villa in Los Angeles. He toured England and performed for King Edward VII at Windsor Castle.

Julian Eltinge debuted at Milwaukee's Alhambra Theater (334 West Wisconsin Avenue) on August 7, 1910. Louise Brand, *Milwaukee Sentinel* reporter, wrote, "Mr. Eltinge not only knows how to make himself look like a beautiful woman, but he knows how to act like one. It did not seem at all ridiculous that all the men on the stage became immediate victims of Eltinge's charms. Men and women on the other side of the footlights did the same thing. Here is a man, who is really so attractive in women's clothes, that the real girls on the stage receive comparatively little to no attention."

Eltinge brought *The Fascinating Widow* to Milwaukee's Davidson Theater (621 North Third Street) in September 1912 and December 1913. He debuted *The Crinoline Girl* at the Davidson in February 1915 and *Cousin Lucy* during Eltinge Week in October 1916. During this spectacle, Eltinge displayed over $10,000 of his gowns and jewelry, offered souvenirs to each female guest and sang a song about "how to eat and grow fat." His movies *The Countess Charming* (believed to be the first representation of drag on film) and *The Clever Mrs. Fairfax* debuted at the Alhambra in 1917 and *The Widow's Might* and *The Son of Democracy* in 1918. In 1919, he appeared in a one-act play at the fabulous Butterfly Theater (212 West Wisconsin Avenue) in April and a Farewell Tour Revue of 1919 at the Davidson Theater in May. Every Eltinge show was a smashing success—often held over days and weeks after the original closing date.

Milwaukee's demand for drag talent was already insatiable by 1920. The "Eltinge Decade" would inspire a legion of local competitors.

McGarvey, female impersonator and dancer, keeps them guessing whether he is a man or a woman at the Orpheum Theater.
—Milwaukee Journal, *December 8, 1913*

Hal Johnson is a female impersonator whose methods are distinctly feminine. His carriage, gestures, sylph-like appearance, and pitch of voice combine to make him a success. A female impersonator who gets away from the established type, and whose work is a real novelty. Mr. Johnson is a Milwaukee boy.
—Milwaukee Sentinel, *February 13, 1914*

Jean Guise, an exceedingly clever female impersonator, is one of the big surprises as well as one of the big hits in the corking good burlesque show presented this week at the Gayety.
—Milwaukee Journal, *December 9, 1915*

If you are one of the wise ones, who cannot be fooled by a female impersonator, do not miss Jean Barrios at the Palace Theater this week. In appearance, voice, and manner, he is an attractive slip of a girl and wears some beautiful gowns.
—Milwaukee Sentinel, *June 10, 1918*

After touring the world, Eltinge headlined Milwaukee Style Week in March 1921 with daily appearances at the Majestic Theater (219 West Wisconsin Avenue). He emceed fashion shows featuring twenty-five living models and Milwaukee's finest couture in four shows daily, complemented by old-school vaudeville comedians, dog acts and even a circus aerialist. While touring on the Orpheum circuit, he visited Milwaukee's Majestic Theater in March 1922 and the Orpheum Palace (535 West Wisconsin Avenue) in April 1923. His films *Madame Behave* opened at the Merrill Theater (211 West Wisconsin Avenue) in February 1926 and *My Caravan* at the Riverside Theater (116 West Wisconsin Avenue) in June 1930. It doesn't appear Eltinge returned to Milwaukee in person after 1923.

With his fame and fortune fleeting, Eltinge was challenged by weight gain, depression and substance abuse. Truth be told, the mother of female impersonation could no longer fit into the glamorous gowns he wore as a "maiden," and his fading feminine wiles had left behind an aged crone.

His 1927 revival show was panned by Los Angeles critics, who said, "Eltinge is a trifle too old and portly to exactly suggest the flapper—his impersonation is now limited to the more matronly of the species."

"No professional calling is so provocative of sneers as that of the female impersonator," wrote O.O. McIntyre in the June 4, 1927 *Milwaukee Sentinel*. "With the exception of Julian Eltinge, few have attained theatrical heights, but even his time is done."

Eltinge could no longer outrun or ignore public sentiment. By eliminating female impersonators, social reformers thought they could also eliminate homosexuals. His last drag appearance in *Maid to Order* (1931) was a box office bomb. The Hays Code, rigidly enforced after 1934, effectively banned homosexual or transvestite representation on the silver screen. With gender impersonation outlawed in Hollywood, there was little left for Eltinge to do.

In 1936, he announced he would no longer perform in female clothing. Despondent, he continued appearing in Hollywood gay clubs—looming especially large over the tiny costumes he once sported in his long-ago shows—while disappointed crowds lamented that his best years were behind him.

Eltinge thought he could survive on his investments, until a 1939 downturn forced him to sell his remarkable villa. Reluctantly, he accepted a New York City nightclub tour in 1941. During an appearance at the Diamond Horseshoe, Eltinge became extremely ill and was sent home. Ten days later, the world's most famous female impersonator died in his apartment on March 7. Although death notices spoke of a kidney ailment, his cause of death was listed as a brain hemorrhage. Some would later claim he died by suicide with sleeping pills.

His will proclaimed, "I declare that I am a bachelor," and left everything to the one woman in his life, his seventy-nine-year-old mother, Julia Dalton. After his death, stories of his closeted gay life abounded for decades.

Multiple directors vowed to film the life story of Eltinge, but in the end, no movie was ever made. Eltinge never even had the chance to perform in his own theater. After a short but scandalous stint as a burlesque house, the Eltinge Theater still stands today on Forty-Second Street as an AMC Empire 25 movie theater.

THE CREOLE FASHION PLATE

Karyl Norman, born George Francis Peduzzi (1897–1947), was another highly influential female impersonator of the late vaudeville era. He was one of several New York–based performers, including Gene Malin and Ray Bourbon, credited with igniting the national "Pansy Craze" of the 1930s.

He was born to an old Baltimore family and traced his heritage back to the West Indies. Despite his lifelong fascination with Creole culture, there is no indication his ancestors were anything but white.

He joined Neil O'Brien's Minstrels in 1913. He moved to the West Coast vaudeville scene, which took him to Australia in 1917. He was known for his two-piano act, his dazzling wardrobe and writing most of his own songs. His mother, Mary Hoffman Peduzzi, was a one-woman costume shop, makeup crew and charm school. Over his thirty-year career, Norman would perform his act on five continents.

Norman quickly became a national celebrity, despite being openly and unapologetically gay. His exotic "Creole" appearance—echoing the vamp looks of Theda Bara—made him the breakout star of any troupe he joined. Actress Fifi D'Orsay described Norman as a "wonderful guy, beloved and respected by everyone, although he was a gay boy." After he was arrested on a morals charge in Detroit, First Lady Eleanor Roosevelt petitioned for his immediate release.

Norman played it straight until he was famous enough not to care, although it often meant being the front face of the scandal sheets. In July 1922, the *Milwaukee Sentinel* reported his arrest for "alleged breach of promise" when he refused to marry former partner and tightrope artist Ruth Budd Carpenter. In turn, Budd sued Norman for $50,000. "I loved her and planned to marry her, but I was marrying her and not her family. A mother-in-law on a honeymoon would have been too much for me," he told gossip reporters, who later turned the tables on him. "The groom-to-be wanted his mamma on the honeymoon too," reported the *Milwaukee Journal* on August 25, 1922. "He simply couldn't get along without her, as she was necessary in looking after his lingerie and buttoning him up the back. After all, Karyl Norman is a well-known feminine impersonator. Read our juicy bit of stage gossip. It's illustrated!"

Vaudevillians found the controversy ridiculous, knowing that Norman was a "Queer Old Fashion Plate."

In January 1923, Norman made his Milwaukee debut selling *Something Different* at the Orpheum Theater (535 West Wisconsin Avenue). Gimbels (101 West Wisconsin Avenue) welcomed him to the sheet music department for live performances and singalongs during his Milwaukee run. He was so popular that he returned several times in the next few years, selling out the house for weeks in the summer of 1923, spring 1924, spring 1925, fall 1925, summer 1927 and summer 1931.

"The girlies are the center of attraction at the Palace Theater this week," said the *Milwaukee Sentinel* on April 7, 1924. "There are several varieties of

Karyl Norman, fascinated with his Caribbean heritage, re-created himself as the "Creole Fashion Plate." *Wisconsin LGBTQ History Project.*

real ones and then there is one almost perfect imitation. We refer to Karyl Norman, whose annual appearance is the signal for all the flappers in the ward. He truly earns the name 'Creole Fashion Plate.' He may be an imitator of the ladies, but there are few who can attempt to imitate him. His act is unique of the kind."

"When Karyl Norman buckles on his armor, so to speak, it consists of the most gorgeous array of gowns, wraps, furs and chapeaux that has ever been sent forth from the world's most celebrated fashion salons," said the *Milwaukee Journal* on April 5, 1925. "Despite the fact that Karyl has played Milwaukee many times, he is still able to fool many persons into believing he is a woman until he pulls the wig. Karyl won more applause than any other act."

"Karyl Norman is today probably the greatest female impersonator on the international stage," said the *Los Angeles Times* in 1925. "His ability to create the illusion of femininity is almost uncanny. He has youth and slenderness, which are merely incidental to his mastery of the gesture, poise and physical features of the deadlier species."

His 1930 Palace Theater act, *Glorifying the American Boy-Girl*, was not only his most popular show ever but also one of the most popular drag shows of the decade. Soon, Norman was headlining New York's Pansy Club (204 West Forty-Eighth Street), an openly queer nightclub operated by organized crime, which allowed female impersonators to come out of the closet for the first time.

Later mentions of Norman were increasingly unkind: an August 1931 *Milwaukee Journal* reference calls him "that man who wears women's clothes and sings about daisies, yeah, you know the one."

Even Dorothy Parker commented, "I was too deeply lost in speculations as to what it would be like to pray for a son, to bring him safely into the world, to watch over him while he ate his carrots and spinach, to see that he wore his rubbers and stood up straight and did his arithmetic, and then have him grow up to be the Creole Fashion Plate."

In the advent of "talkies," vaudeville declined from main attraction to intermission fodder. Norman moved to Los Angeles and hostessed at Club La Boheme. His signature act was Joan Crawford from *Rain*, an act that received Crawford's in-person applause and approval. After La Boheme closed in 1933, he opened the Karyl Norman Supper Club and continued his traveling shows.

While drag was being criminalized across America, Norman was performing nightly at Finocchio's in San Francisco throughout 1937. He returned to the Riverside Theater in the summer of 1937 with the vaudeville revival Esquire Sketches.

The *Milwaukee Sentinel* quipped, "The old vaudeville favorite, Karyl Norman, has noticeably increased his weight." A New York reporter added, "For some years, there was Karyl Norman, the Creole Fashion Plate, and I recall what a dashing exotic woman he was…and how disappointed I was when I met him one day without his feminine get-up to find an ordinary looking young man."

Reluctantly aging, Norman was deeply hurt by the bad press. He retreated from the stage to run a short-lived vaudeville club on Long Island. His mother passed away in 1938, leaving him alone in the world for the very first time, which triggered a long bout of depression. He vowed to retire, but it doesn't seem he ever actually did. According to his World War II draft card, he was working at Detroit's famous Club Frontenac in 1940. He returned to touring in 1942 with an All American Male Revue in Lima, Ohio, and toured Australia in 1946. He promised reporters a comeback—as a Lena Horne impersonator—but that never came.

In 1947, Norman accepted a job at the Ha Ha Club in Hollywood, Florida. He died on July 23, 1947, of heart disease at only fifty years old.

THE GIRL-MAN OF MILWAUKEE

On May 2, 1914, Ralph Kerwineo was arrested by Milwaukee police. The official charge was disorderly conduct, but the accusation was that he was biologically, in fact, she.

For thirteen years, Ralph had effectively lived his life as a man. He was described as the perfect gentleman, well dressed and well educated, and among the finest sportsmen known in Milwaukee. He worked in men-only jobs at the Plankinton Hotel, Gimbels and Cutler-Hammer.

Ralph informally married Mamie White in Chicago in 1906, but he couldn't limit himself to just one woman. The relationship was long riddled with affairs, and Mamie grew tired of Ralph's smoking, drinking, cursing and gambling. In 1914, Ralph obtained a groom's health certificate and legally married his mistress, Dorothy Kleinowski. When Mamie found out, she went straight to the police and outed Ralph as a "cross-dresser."

The case attracted negative national attention. Ralph was immediately labeled as a deviant who "impersonated" a man to take advantage of a confused woman. Called to trial, Ralph appealed to the judge to understand how much easier it was to find gainful employment in industrial Milwaukee as a man. "We had been subject to all sorts of overtures from all kinds and conditions of men....If I assumed men's clothes, I would be better able to obtain work, and as a 'man,' I could protect my 'wife' from insult."

It was a brilliant defense. Surprisingly, Milwaukee was very supportive of Ralph. The chief of police was quick to state, "There is no moral perversion in this case." Reporters commented that Ralph was just trying to make a honest living, support his wife and be a respected citizen, just like

After two-timing his wife, Ralph Kerwineo was outed as the "Girl-Man of Milwaukee." *Wisconsin LGBTQ History Project.*

any other working man. People almost forgot Ralph was not a biological man. Almost.

Although the charges were dropped, Ralph was misgendered through the trial and ultimately ordered to wear female attire and use his birth name.

"They are writing the last chapter of the life of Ralph Kerwineo," said the defendant. "When we leave this courtroom, Kerwineo will be dead." His new wife soon left him, saying, "As a man I loved her, but when she donned skirts that love died."

For a while, Ralph seems to have rejected the judge's orders. He capitalized on his reputation as the "Girl-Man of Milwaukee" and joined the Orpheum vaudeville scene. Ralph toured the country as a public speaker about his experience. In 1915, he was arrested in Racine for "masquerading as a man," and in 1919, he was released on probation after police found him in bed with a woman. By the 1920s, audiences were bored with Kerwineo, and many began to view him again as a huckster and con man.

"I thought of myself as a man, and it never entered my mind that I was any different than the men around me with whom I laughed, joked, worked and played my part," said Ralph.

Ralph relocated to Chicago, where, living as Cora, he later married Jacob Seifert. He died on October 4, 1932, and is buried in Lake View Cemetery.

THE GIRL-BANDIT OF CHICAGO

Newspapers were still mourning Burt Savoy even as a strange new scandal erupted in Chicago. On June 21, 1923, the *Milwaukee Journal* printed a shocking headline: "'Girl-Bandit' Is Husband, Wife at Same Time," chronicling the sensational murder trial of Chicago financier Richard Tesmer. As it turned out, the accused female bandit (Frances Carrick) was not a woman but a man born Fred Thompson. The article elaborated:

> *Thomas faced his interrogators, still clad in the black gown, silk stockings, and high-heeled slippers he wore when arrested, although now a two-day*

growth of beard has penetrated the powder and rouge. Neighbors knew Thompson as a model wife. Children living on the block called him Aunt Frances. He was recently a hostess at a party. Pastries and salads that he made himself were described as delicious.

With twists and turns nearly impossible to believe, the story of Frances Carrick (1888–1953) fascinated Milwaukee newspaper readers for weeks. Carrick somehow managed two Chicago brothels under assumed names, while living with legal husband, Frank, and legal wife, Marie Clark, in a polyamorous, heroin-addicted household.

Even stranger than her genderfluid existence, even more dubious than her bigamous marriages, Carrick had previously assumed the identity of May Belmont, a mysteriously missing 1890s minstrel show headliner. In June 1913, the second May Belmont was arrested in Syracuse, New York, after a "peeping Tom" (more likely, sex customer) reported that she was a female impersonator. During her imprisonment, Carrick was subjected to a full body search that revealed "the caged songbird is indeed masculine." In response, Carrick admitted to being arrested five times in the past, without anyone ever suspecting his true self.

Ten years later, Richard Tesmer was murdered in Chicago by a woman with an "evil, leering, Satanic grin." After identifying eight other women as the killer, eyewitness Mrs. Tesmer proclaimed Frances Carrick the culprit. "My God! That is the girl who murdered my husband," she announced

Frances Carrick lived outside the law—and far, far outside gender expectations. *Milwaukee Public Library.*

after police raided Carrick's home and arrested the entire household. The Chicago Police hoped that the court would condemn Carrick, a cross-dressing deviant, so they could close the case.

News reporters focused more on Carrick's fashions, mannerisms and theatrical behavior than the actual legal proceedings. They were startled by her "womanliness" and her "sexual allure," but most of all, they were fascinated by her lack of facial hair. She was called a "psychic hermaphrodite," a "man-girl" and a "third-sexer," but never did reporters use the negative language of the era (e.g., "invert," "pervert," "degenerate") to describe her. She was a local sensation with a legion of admirers (mostly gay men) who faithfully followed her every word. People wrote to Carrick from all over the country asking, but she never revealed her secret formula for hair removal. Reporters shared her thoughtful quotes; photographers stopped by for stage-worthy snapshots. One of them, "The Shaving Grace," made the national news syndicate. In response, the prison warden—who had tolerated Carrick's request to wear female clothing—demanded that she wear male clothing in the future.

Chicago papers certainly tuned in when Carrick threatened to write a book about the secret lives of her bordello customers. "A lot of prominent guys in this city will die when they hear about me being a man," she said, defiantly. However, no book was ever written.

The Carrick trial had two shocking outcomes: first, the judge dismissed the testimony of Frank Carrick, stating that a husband could not legally testify against his wife (even if that wife were legally recognized as a man), and second, Frances Carrick was found not guilty after a two-hour jury determination. Both verdicts were totally unexpected: same-sex marriages didn't exist in 1923 and couldn't be recognized as legal, nor could the provisions of marriage extend themselves to a same-sex couple. Somehow, Carrick triumphed, and photographs show her surrounded by applauding fans. The Tesmer murder was never solved.

Although she claimed she was going back to a quiet country life, Carrick accepted a $500-per-week contract to perform risqué gender-play shows at the Rialto. The Chicago Police and mayor, outraged at the verdict, certainly weren't going to let her get rich at their expense. They applied pressure on the theater, which was "catering to perverted minds" with its "indecent spectacle." The Rialto eventually broke the contract, and Frances Carrick vanished from history.

The story of Frances Carrick tantalized and slightly terrified Milwaukee. It signified, once again, that onstage gender play was making a leap to offstage life—and inviting vice and scandal into the lives of respectable people. While queer people saw Carrick a heroine, the moral takeaway for the mainstream remained never trust a deceiver.

THE UNINHIBITION OF PROHIBITION

"What's become of all the female impersonators?" asked Ted Cook, a *Milwaukee Sentinel* columnist, on April 28, 1928. "There aren't any left, even among the women."

"Between you and me," wrote a *Milwaukee Journal* reporter on May 24, 1928, "it's the amazing invasion of half man, half woman freaks that is causing the most trouble on the midway....The good people who pay their dimes have found this freak a particularly alluring one."

Across the United States, Prohibition created an underground scene where creative artists, musicians, actors and thrill-seekers connected in large numbers. Mafia-operated nightspots allowed both questioning and confirmed to express themselves in new and exhilarating ways. National stars like Jean Malin and Gladys Bentley didn't even pretend they were straight—they simply didn't care about the consequences. The Pansy Craze was everything we'd ever heard about the Roaring Twenties except shot through a vibrant lavender lens.

By 1930, *Variety* reported, there were thirty-five "pansy parlors" in Towertown, the neighborhood near the Old Chicago Water Tower.

"Tough Chicago has [an] epidemic of male butterflies," wrote the *Chicago Tribune* on December 9, 1930. "The world's toughest town, Chicago, is going pansy. And liking it."

Milwaukee, on a smaller scale, enjoyed the craze while it lasted.

SCANDALS AT THE ST. CHARLES HOTEL

At 1:30 a.m. on June 1, 1928, the St. Charles Hotel (786 North Water Street) in Milwaukee's City Hall Square was the scene of a spectacular Prohibition raid that blew the top off the town.

Milwaukee was eight years into Prohibition, but you wouldn't know it from the scene at the St. Charles. The U.S. district attorney reported, "We have absolute evidence that liquor was sold promiscuously at the hotel. We have evidence that booze was sold in at least 20 rooms. This is the heaviest

Prohibition amplified Milwaukee's Pansy Craze at hotspots like the St. Charles Hotel.
Milwaukee Public Library.

padlock the government has ever asked for in Wisconsin." Federal judge F.A. Geiger remarked, "There appears to have been no difficulty whatsoever in getting liquor here."

The St. Charles was popular for other reasons, as the agents reported the behavior of the "lewd chorus girls from the Gayety Theater." One agent reported that uninvited performers came into his room, made themselves at home and drank gin freely. "You could have liquor parties in the St. Charles Hotel any night you wanted them, with chorus girls attending. All you had to do was call the desk and order a bottle. Gin was delivered immediately. Persons prominent in Milwaukee's social circles had parties there."

Cocktails often led to reckless abandon. One agent recounted, "The girls came to my room for drinks wearing only kimonos, step-ins, shoes or smiles, and often turned handstands or somersaults on the floor. Some of the girls may have been boys." When cross-examined, the agent admitted that he had never asked the girls to leave or stop their naked gymnastics.

Prohibition agents used curious language to describe the crowds at these St. Charles Hotel parties. "Bull daggers and pansy boys haunt the [St. Charles] hallways," reads one report. "Degenerates will find doors open to them here." Through these reports, the St. Charles Hotel became known as a safe gathering place for gays and lesbians—one of the first ever documented in Milwaukee.

The St. Charles Hotel and over $410,000 of property were padlocked and seized for one year from July 11, 1928. It was the largest hotel ever padlocked as a dry law nuisance in the United States.

Seventy-one permanent guests were ultimately thrown out of their rooms and became refuges. One year later, the padlocks came off the St. Charles Hotel, which reopened on July 19, 1929, under the same management. Incredibly, seventy of the seventy-one former guests reclaimed their dust-covered rooms. But the dust never really settled for the St. Charles.

On October 8, 1931, the St. Charles Hotel went dark. Following a federal indictment, near bankruptcy, a sensational divorce and a series of supernatural events, manager Joseph Budar had seen and heard enough.

Budar transferred to the Royal Hotel (435 West Michigan) and took most of his staff and residents with him. Local papers commented about the "circus caravan procession" that ensued, as guests dragged their trunks, luggage and furniture down Water and Michigan Streets to their new home.

Only five years old, the Royal Hotel was already a girl down on her luck. One might even say the hotel was cursed. After losing his wife to suicide and his daughter to estrangement, owner Royal Nixdorf—who had envisioned the Royal as the first in a national chain of Royal Hotels—lost the hotel in the Great Depression. From reopening day in 1929 onward, the hotel was the scene of continual police activity.

Beneath this smoky cover, the Royal quickly became known as a place where gay, lesbian and gender nonconforming people could comingle freely and without fear. Longtime hotel manager Mabel Myers Leviash would cover legal charges for anyone arrested for "sexual perversion" on the

For four decades before Stonewall, the Royal Hotel was a queer refuge. *Milwaukee Public Library.*

property. There were many, because the Royal Hotel bar and lower-level restrooms were notorious cruising grounds from the 1930s to the 1970s, and by 1972, it was the center of Milwaukee's drag community.

THE COMING OF THE DRAG CABARETS

Jean Malin's death on August 10, 1933, is often considered the end of the national Pansy Craze, but Milwaukee was a bit behind the national trend. As Milwaukee emerged from Prohibition in 1933, there was significant concern about a return to the lawlessness of the Roaring Twenties. When the 12:30 a.m. curfew was temporarily lifted in November 1933, Milwaukee saw an explosion of midnight-to-dawn clubs of dubious moral quality. Many of these bars were staffed with "B-girls" whose job was to stimulate heavy spending by any means necessary.

The *Milwaukee Sentinel* led a twilight tour of "gay clubs, locked nightspots and low dives" in a series titled "Lights Burn Brightest Long After Curfew." From "nose-dive" shots at the Tennessee Club (721 West St. Paul Avenue) to pushy female escorts at the Roseland (1224 North Water Street), the reporter ultimately found himself at Club La Tosca (516 East Detroit Street, now St. Paul).

> *La Tosca is patronized by a better class of night club enthusiasts. It's a club, but membership cards are not necessary for entrance. A greenback is a far more effective passport through the door and straight into the welcoming smile of Peggy, the hat check girl. The floor show is on, and she extols the performance. It's something unusual for Milwaukee: female impersonators.*
>
> *There is little embarrassment on that score after highballs have mellowed the drinkers. Guests continue to arrive at this late hour. In some secluded corners, drinking, dancing, and dining are neglected as persons exchange embraces. It is true that after 1 a.m., Club La Tosca really gets into some heavy business. The smoke and noise don't abate until thousands of Milwaukeeans have already finished breakfast and are set off to work.*

Among Club La Tosca's youngest starlets was Billie Herrero (1918–1992), who became one of the world's first international drag superstars as "the Brazilian Carmen Miranda," the "Brazilian Gypsy Rose Lee" and "Senorita Herrero, the Brazilian Sensation."

Debaucherous drag cabarets, like Club La Tosca, began to concern the moral authorities. *Milwaukee Public Library.*

Soon, Club La Tosca wasn't the only venue featuring female impersonators. The College Inn (164 West Wisconsin Avenue) and the Bon Ton (206 East Juneau Avenue) began offering nightly shows in 1933.

By June 1934, the Chez Paree (4507 West Wisconsin Avenue) had become the talk of the town, offering the *Boys Will Be Girls* drag show three times a night, six nights a week, with an extra raunchy "late show" that started at 2:30 a.m.

Owner Joseph Budar, formerly the manager of the Fountain Inn, the Palm Garden and the St. Charles and Royal Hotels, was well known for supporting queer people. His secret to maintaining a mixed crowd was "always free champagne" before, during and after the show. The Chez Paree offered a dance hall with a full brass orchestra five nights a week. The club was also known for its eight-course dinners for just one dollar. It was inspired by a glamorous Chicago nightclub of the same name.

Chez Paree moved way out to Twentieth and Rawson in 1937 to avoid increasing pressure from Milwaukee police. By June 1940, a bankrupt Budar had been forced to sell the Chez Paree to new owners. While the Chicago Chez Paree stayed open until 1960, it seems Milwaukee's Chez Paree closed sometime in 1946. It was still offering drag shows in its final summer—something that had become illegal in most U.S. cities.

The Nut House (623 North Sixth Street) was the most notorious nightspot of the era. Offering a nightly Pansies on Parade revue headlined by Nina Mae McKinney, the Nut House exploded racial, sexual and gender norms in a self-proclaimed "mess of misbehavior." "It's an unusual attraction—and a startling revue—the whole town is talking about the NUT HOUSE," said the ads.

Miss Sophie Uzelac, proprietor, modeled her bar after Eddie Freed's Nut House (550 North Clark Street), a "gay night spot resort" in Chicago, which proudly featured ebony and pansy shows. By February 1935, the Nut House was called "nothing more than a rendezvous for female impersonators" by local newspapers. After undercover investigators attended a weekend of Nut House shows, they vowed to shut down the "depravity."

"Pansy shows aren't what the Milwaukee city fathers consider proper tavern entertainment, said Joseph Drewniak, deputy police inspector. "Men should be men."

The Common Council threatened to outlaw female impersonators completely. "We don't want Milwaukee to go the way of Chicago," warned a councilman. Owner Sophie Uzelac was forced to change to a "black and tan" format to keep her license. The Nut House remained open until December 1935, but the shows never really stopped.

The police successfully harassed the Bon Ton into closing later in 1935. By that time, the College Inn had already closed. It was replaced by the Red Room Bar in the Plankinton Arcade, which established its own reputation as a go-to gay landmark throughout the 1940s and 1950s.

THE GREAT REJECTION

Drag was quickly falling out of favor. Middle America was beginning to worry about the "deception" of gender play, as seen in a February 5, 1933 *Milwaukee Journal* article, "Masquerade of Sex Queer Human Trait":

"The impulse to masquerade—to misrepresent one's sex—has given history innumerable romances of impersonation. A woman who disguises herself as a man, or a man who poses as a woman, conceivably may carry out the deception over many years, providing they stay out of trouble and do not bump up against the law," wrote the unnamed author, who cited James Blunt, Millie Brown and Martha Frances McDonald as examples of those who learned a lesson for their deception. "The police do not look kindly on impersonators….Science says that persons of that kind are not normal. Police admit that more impersonators are at large than generally comes to public notice, because it is only when arrests are made that exposure follows."

"As a rule, the female impersonator is a pronounced masculine type. One peculiarly enough graduated to his calling from the driver's seat of a truck. Most are married, but they live pretty much alone. They are conscious of a certain stigma."

Although Hoyt Bill sterilizations were relatively slow prior to 1932, something certainly changed that year. Most of the forced sterilizations in Wisconsin history happened between 1932 and 1934, at the height of the Pansy Craze pushback. A shocking 570 Wisconsin residents were sterilized during that two-year window. The statute remained on Wisconsin lawbooks until 1978.

The Great Depression was crushing nightlife faster than any police force or public sentiment. As few could afford leisure travel, Chicago's Century of Progress didn't bring the expected economic boom to the Chicago-Milwaukee corridor. Queer nightlife paid a tremendous price in both cities.

Female impersonators were such an economic concern that even the Cooks and Waiters Union called for a ban. "Female impersonators and singing waiters are a menace as grave as the 'come-on maidens,'" wrote the union on November 17, 1934. "They scab upon both the entertainer and the waiter. The Council must take some action about this unfair competition."

As police began to crack down on the gender nonconforming, any liberties the gay community had assumed during the Pansy Craze were quickly taken back.

In September 1932, police raided a West Side hobo camp in search of a "womanish man" reported to be living in the "jungle." She was Martha Frances McDonald, from Edmund, North Dakota. Found wearing men's overalls and leather boots and sporting a boy's haircut, she was sent to the House of Correction for thirty days. Soon after release, she was arrested again for working (as a man) in a South Side railroad yard. After another sixty-day sentence, she was released on the grounds that she leave the city immediately. "The woman tramp hasn't been seen since," said police, "and we are all the more comfortable for it."

On August 6, 1934, Joseph Tomczak, twenty-five, of 2227 South Seventeenth Street, was apprehended at Water and State for "wearing the complete apparel of a woman." He confided that he had been living as a woman for several years with his husband, Leroy Massey. After a psychological evaluation found him to be sane, Tomczak was fined five dollars and ordered to "present properly in public." Massey was discovered to be a deserter from the Fort Benning, Georgia barracks and remanded to U.S. Army custody.

"One wonders what Julian Eltinge, back on Broadway for a looksee, thinks of the flock of degenerately rouged and smirking female impersonators for which he blazed [a] trail," asked the *Milwaukee Sentinel* on October 12, 1934.

"The gradual decline of the female impersonator has come to a full stop," said the *Milwaukee Sentinel* on April 4, 1935. "Such performers cannot be booked save in remote sections of honky-tonks. Even a burlesque of the idea gets the bird. The fact is these androgynous antics have always proved precarious. Deservedly or not, moderns began to look on female impersonators as pathetically psychopathic."

Society was now convinced that female impersonators were sexual deviants. Between 1935 and 1937, female impersonators were outlawed in Chicago, New York, Baltimore, Boston, New Orleans, Los Angeles, Philadelphia, Cleveland, Atlantic City and many other cities. They continued to perform on the fringes—Key West, Las Vegas, Provincetown, Canadian and Mexican border towns—although it was dangerous to do so.

San Francisco became a national refuge for banished performers, as did Detroit, where Club Frontenac, the Gold Dollar and the Diplomat remained top drag destinations. "Female impersonators and beef-trust gals have a stranglehold on Detroit's nightlife," commented the *Detroit Herald* on March 9, 1937.

By the mid-1930s, female impersonators were back to being seen as circus folk. Arvin Giese, seventeen, of Brillion, Wisconsin, wanted to be famous. After much reflection and the advice of villagers, he sought to become a female impersonator. Weighing 541 pounds, the "Blue-Eyed Behemoth" toured six states as the man-baby "Sonny Boy" in summer 1933. Wearing a wig and a hula skirt, he performed numerous musical numbers at local taverns and Lion's Club shows.

"Fatty, as he has been known since childhood, is rapidly achieving mastodon proportions. He eats eight times a day—and pork and potatoes are his favorite foods. Onstage, his tremendous thighs shake with mirth. The great folds of fat on his body quiver as he steps through the dance. When he puts on his best sweet smile, the women in the audience titter," said the *Milwaukee Journal*. "Giese is a panic who knocks them right out of their seats."

"There burns a fierce ambition to make something of himself," said the April 8, 1934 *Milwaukee Journal*. "He wants to get a position at the Chicago World's Fair. He vows that he is going to Hollywood within a year." Ultimately, Arvin Giese chose his family tavern over fame and fortune. He died in February 1981 at age sixty-four.

BEWARE THE MORON MENACE

Tabloid newspapers shifted their focus from out-of-control immorality to violent sex crimes, which were supposedly victimizing women and girls of all ages across the country. People were encouraged to beware the "sex moron"—inverted homosexuals who could not control their unnatural sexual urges and might become peeping Toms, rapists, child molesters and murderers. This firestorm of homosexual panic was fanned by none other than J. Edgar Hoover and the FBI, which attributed multiple unsolved sex crimes to gay men in the late 1930s.

"Danger! One thousand escaped feeble-minded and insane persons… most of them capable of bestial sex crimes…are at large in Chicago!" warned the *Chicago American*. Chicago's city council even passed a law that required "moron alarms" on fire escapes to warn about home intruders.

The "Moron Menace" broadcast a national message that homosexuality was a mental disease and that homosexuals were extremely dangerous. Although crime had increased in some cities, the crimes weren't being perpetrated by gay men—nor did it really make any sense that gay men would be violating women and small girls. Reformers started pushing for much stronger, much more exclusionary laws against gay people. Michigan and Illinois passed sexual psychopath laws that had devastating effect on human lives. This reaction was so swift and severe that this era (1936–1946) is now known to historians as the "Post-Pansy Panic."

"No man ever wants to be a woman, nor to be mistaken for one," said the *Milwaukee Sentinel*. "To be called sissy is a fight word, and off the vaudeville stage, no man assumes the role of the female impersonator. Many women parade the street in britches, but you will NEVER see a man diked out in décolleté ball gown."

"If women dressed to please men, you would never see another female in britches," countered the *Milwaukee Journal*. "For men feel about the woman who gets herself up as an imitation man, just exactly as women feel about a man who is a female impersonator. There is nothing alluring to a man about a woman who looks like a grubby little boy."

The legacy of the Pansy Craze was a far more focused—but unfortunately, far more regulated—sense of personal sexual identity. "Most people began thinking of themselves as either hetero- or homosexual, while a century ago, people did not think of themselves or organize their emotional lives through those categories," said historian Chad Heap. At the same time, media campaigns sought to squash any pride these newfound identities inspired.

Milwaukee's one and only mention of a menacing moron came in 1939. On March 10 of that year, Rosetta Silverman was followed to her home at Eighth and North Avenue. The stranger, wearing a dark coat of rich material, a high collar and a large plumed hat, asked her which way was Seventh Street. As Rosetta began to walk away, the masher said, "Just a minute, girlie," and grabbed her roughly and improperly. After the incident, she ran home, and the lady vanished. Police told neighbors to beware a stranger with an "unskilled voice and unladylike walk" who was "at least 40 years old, with an out of fashion hat like that."

As World War II rolled around, the only mention of female impersonators was the rumor that they were infiltrating the army and pretending to be nurses.

"As far as I know, San Francisco is now the only major city with a nightclub or floor show featuring female impersonators," said Ev Durling, *Milwaukee Journal* "On the Side" writer, on November 16, 1942.

But not for long.

3

INTO THE JEWEL BOX (1937–1960)

Sodom, Gomorrah and Monte Carlo all rolled into one, that is Miami.
—Miami Herald, *1929*

Even as the Pansy Craze came to a screeching halt and drag was criminalized around America over the next five years, the greatest generation of female impersonation was being born in Florida.

And it would have a profound effect on Milwaukee for generations.

It was an unbelievable pitch for the 1930s. Danny Brown and Doc (Frank W.) Benner, a gay couple on the down low, sought to rescue the art of drag from the shadowy, vice-ridden corners of bordellos, burlesque halls and "pansy parties"; book shows with profitable venues, respectable audiences and straight customers; and conquer the nation—even the world—as the world's first racially and sexually diverse traveling troupe of female impersonators.

And it was entirely gay-owned and operated.

The couple met between 1932 and 1934 at the Jungle Nate Club in Youngstown, Ohio, where Brown was a master of ceremonies and Benner was a dancer. Shows were quite clearly gay-friendly, with names like Gay Boy Girl Revue, Boys Will Be Girls Revue, All Star Collegiate Male Revue, Glorifying the American Boy and, finally, Danny Brown & His Female Impersonators. After launching a series of "original male" and "gay boy girl" traveling shows, they opened the first Jewel Box Club in the Embassy

Hotel in South Beach in 1936. The first official Jewel Box Revue tour was in 1937. Danny and Doc planned to spend summers on tour and spend winters at their cabaret.

Brown and Benner's touring strategy was inspiring: they bravely booked shows at high-end, respectable nightclubs, African American theaters, small-town community theaters and even gay-friendly venues. The Jewel Box Revue inspired a national network of drag destinations in America's largest cities and restored a national appetite for drag entertainment.

FINOCCHIO'S (1929–1979)

Despite offering drag shows for seven decades, Finocchio's was never really a gay-friendly destination. The club capitalized on its gay performers for amusement—even the name Finocchio's is negative Italian slang for homosexual—but its owners never really wanted to deal with gay customers. While Joe Finocchio (1898–1986) provided gainful employment to generations of gay men who might otherwise struggle to survive in San Francisco, he was always more interested in running a profitable tourist attraction than a LGBTQ safe space, social outlet or historic landmark. In 1929, he guarded the door at his father's speakeasy, which offered underground drag shows for a dime.

"I knew some famous female impersonators," Finocchio told the *Los Angeles Times* in 1984. "And I got an idea. If I can get the right talent, I'm going to start a place of my own. I knew there was big business."

Remarkably, Finocchio's never attracted negative police attention, although it was (begrudgingly) a known gay gathering place. San Francisco's police chief declared war on female impersonators in 1936 and arrested five performers during a highly publicized raid. After that, Finocchio's was never raided again.

Joe's first wife, Marjorie, was the front face of the operation: booking entertainers, directing shows, furnishing the nightclub. Robin Raye, an impersonator who performed at the Garden of Allah, Finocchio's and the Jewel Box Revue, said of Marge Finocchio, "I don't think she liked gay people, but she certainly knew how to use them."

"I made $150 a week, and that was the most we could make in those days," said Raye. "It was not worth having to cope with Mrs. Finocchio's unending power trip. She would expect people to say goodnight to her—and her dog—every night, but I wouldn't do it. 'I hear you've been saying things behind my back,' she said, and I snapped back, 'I haven't said anything, Mrs. Finocchio, because you're not interesting enough for me to talk about.'"

"They thought I was crazy to turn down this work," said Raye. "But Marge Finocchio made millions off drag queens. Millions. We made that woman rich."

The club's longstanding policy of "come as a boy, leave as a boy" meant that performers weren't allowed to be seen offstage in drag. They were not allowed to mingle with the audience whatsoever. Employees referred to Finocchio's as the "House of Hate," where workers were labeled as Pets or Pests. Performers were hired and fired on a whim. "You could not mix with the customers," said a performer. "All you could do is sit back in the dressing room and fight with each other."

During the 1939 Golden Gate International Exposition, Finocchio's achieved national popularity rare for nightclubs of that era. It was seen as a symbol of San Francisco's cultural sophistication.

"People accept our show more as pure entertainment than they did in the past. They see it as an artistry, rather than a perversion," said Finocchio. "It is entirely different from what they were thinking."

Tourists kept coming—as many as 300,000 per year—and they kept Finocchio's in the green for decades. "America's Most Unusual Nightclub" was the West Coast destination for drag entertainment and drag opportunities, attracting Hollywood celebrities and aspiring female impersonators alike. At its peak, the club offered four shows a night, six days a week, and employed nearly one hundred performers.

After Joe's death, his second wife, Eve, and grandson Eric kept the San Francisco tradition running for another thirteen years. As demand for old-school drag dwindled, Eve announced Finocchio's would be closing on November 27, 1999, due to a substantial rent increase. Although it was their first increase in fifteen years, profit margins had become precariously slim.

"Joe felt he was giving the customer something different," she told the *San Francisco Chronicle*. "It was all clean entertainment, nothing to be ashamed of. People weren't sure what they were going to get when they came in, but they went out laughing.

"I can't imagine Finocchio's not being in San Francisco, but honey, that's the way it goes." After seventy years in business, Finocchio's went dark without even a grand finale show. Eve Finocchio died in 2007.

WONDER CLUB/CLUB MY-O-MY (c. 1933–1972)

Female impersonators couldn't be found on New Orleans's Bourbon Street in the 1930s, when the Wonder Bar (125 Decatur Street) began running underground drag shows. In 1936, proprietor Emile Morlet appealed for relief from police raids, saying they were ruining his business. The city attorney refused to intervene, citing the Wonder Bar as a "menace to morals."

After being harassed out of the French Quarter, the Wonder Bar reopened on the shores of Lake Pontchartrain as Wonder Club. The club was built on pilings over the lake, at the Jefferson-Orleans Parish line, which Morlet understood to be outside New Orleans police jurisdiction.

By the late 1940s, the bar was operating as Club My-O-My. The My-O-My proudly presented the "world's most beautiful boys in women's attire" in "New Orleans' claim to the unusual." The owners attracted traveling shows to complement their popular house cast. "The most interesting women are not women at all. They are Club My-O-My's accomplished female impersonators," read the programs.

The club was badly damaged in a May 4, 1948 fire. Owners rebuilt on the same location, but the My-O-My was destroyed by a second fire on January 17, 1972.

THE 181 CLUB (1945–1953)

"Who's No Lady?" asked the ads, featuring exotic female and male impersonators in stunning outfits. Truth be told, it was often difficult to know. Even more difficult was knowing who, if anyone, was actually homosexual in a nightclub that catered to straights.

The 181 Club (181 Second Avenue) was so posh that customers called it the "homosexual Copacabana." The New York nightclub featured three shows a night, six nights a week, with tuxedoed lesbian serviettes that drew women in large numbers. The strange mix of mobsters, tourists, village locals, slumming socialites and drag chasers enjoyed "The East Side's Gayest Spot" for eight years. Eventually, it lost its liquor license after being labeled a "hangout for perverts of both sexes." After its closure, Anna Genovese opened Club 82, only a few blocks away.

CLUB 82 (1953–1973)

New York drag history dates to the Harlem balls of the 1860s and the Slide (157 Bleecker Street), a fairy resort of the 1890s that featured "inhuman and unnatural" drag shows. By the 1920s, high-end drags were attracting up to seven thousand attendees.

Not to be outdone by the "25 Boys and 1 Girl" of the Jewel Box Revue, Club 82 offered the largest drag shows ever seen in America. It was "New York's After-Dark Rendezvous"—and it was outrageous.

By the 1950s, the Genovese crime family operated most Greenwich Village gay bars, despite laws that made it illegal to serve or host homosexuals at a licensed business. "The law made the gay bars illegal," said an anonymous eyewitness. "The family made it operable."

Operated by the bisexual Anna Genovese, Club 82 was a sexually flirtatious speakeasy that catered exclusively to straight customers. Souvenir photographs were sold at the club, but morally upright patrons were often afraid of people finding out they had been there. As a result, souvenir programs, matchbooks, table drummers and photos are extremely rare and highly coveted by collectors.

Management had inhuman expectations of the cast, which performed three Broadway-level productions every night, in glamorous gowns from designer John Wong. Orchestra leader Johnny Wilson and Carnegie-trained show director Kit Russel didn't allow anyone to miss even one beat. Liberace, Burt Lancaster, Judy Garland, Frank Sinatra, Elizabeth Taylor, Tennessee Williams and other celebrities behaved badly. It was the type of place where a drunken Errol Flynn might play the piano—with his male member—onstage at two o'clock in the morning.

The cast was almost entirely gay, but it was not a gay-friendly place. Cross-dressing was illegal at the time, and performers were expected to leave their Club 82 identities behind when they left the stage. Like the Jewel Box, the performers used male pronouns and "Mister" titles to deflect any suspicion of "deception" or "deviance." Gender was strictly policed: men were required to look like men when they entered and exited the bar. Half of this was proprietary: the club "owned" its performers, so they weren't allowed to moonlight at other venues. The other half was profiteering: if audiences suspected the performers were deviants who wanted to be women, they wouldn't return.

Club 82 offered virtually no protections for its customers or cast. Female impersonators competed from all over the country to work here, only to find an exhausting, exploitative and cruel workplace. "Working in that club killed a part of me," performer Toby Marsh said in 2012. "Whatever little innocence I had left, died there."

Club 82 was also a segregated floor show. The cast was white, the audience was white and the staff was white. The club remained relevant only if upper-class, straight white customers kept coming. By the late 1960s, homosexuals were chasing equality, not chasing meager tips from a bridge-and-tunnel audience. Drag bars were no longer seen as exotic or subversive but an appropriation of gay culture. As the East Village became more dangerous, Club 82 had trouble filling tables. In 1972, the curtain fell for the last time without any hoopla at all.

THE GARDEN OF ALLAH (1946–1956)

World War II liberated a closeted America from silence, isolation and self-contempt. Many flocked to coastal towns where they could live freely, independently and outside the expectations of small-town life.

As the Pacific Northwest's first gay-owned and operated business, Seattle's Garden of Allah attracted gay men and lesbians in large numbers. Located in the basement speakeasy of the Arlington Hotel in Pioneer Square, the Garden of Allah put the "Queen" in the Queen City with cutting-edge drag shows, vaudeville, burlesque and cabaret talent. Magicians, jugglers, singers, comedians, even dog trainers hosted shows over the years. In the 1930s, the Arlington Hotel bar allowed openly gay men and women to gather here and even booked clandestine drag shows. After the Jewel Box's opening night appearance in 1946, the Garden of Allah came out as the Northwest's number-one destination for female impersonators.

Blending Middle Eastern exoticism, Arab fantasies and gender illusion, the Garden was a risqué, anonymous and down low space with relaxed gender rules. People came to see the female impersonators from a safe distance, careful not to mix with the "fairies" and "dykes" among the bar's regulars.

Jackie Starr, one of the first national drag stars, started doing drag in New York's Mafia speakeasies in 1929. She was recruited for a grand tour of South America and Europe, where she was promised an empire by a prince later killed in World War II. She dated senators and congressmen in Washington, D.C., where she always packed a razor to shave the morning after so she could leave their homes under the cover of perfect femininity. She joined the Jewel Box Revue in 1938, danced as a Rockette at Radio City, joined the war, married a woman and fathered a child, all before arriving in Seattle in 1946. She was far past her peak when she headlined the Garden of Allah, but she held that title for ten full years.

Slowly but surely, the Garden of Allah became a tired old tourist trap.

"It was a dark old Grand Victorian hotel that had lost its luster," remembered a patron. "You would pass one dollar through a peephole, like they used to do in the 1920s. I remember a warbling Wurlitzer organ, dark stained wood accents, off-white tile floors, all of which was so out of style by the 1950s. They were so busy, they'd just empty ashtrays on the floor."

Owners Frank Reid and Fred Coleman sought to create not only an entertainment venue but also a support network for gay, lesbian and gender nonconforming pioneers. Loyal customers sought to create a local tourist destination for gay visitors. Historians would later credit the Garden of Allah for sparking a collective LGBTQ consciousness for the first time. Still, it had its critics.

"[Reid and Coleman] made a lot of money at the Garden of Allah—and they took every nickel home with them," said performer Roby Jacome.

By the 1950s, there were over a dozen gay bars and businesses within walking distance, including the legendary Double Header (1933–2015). The Garden was under attack in its final years, with gay bar raids, drag queen arrests, random shutdowns and an ever-intrusive police presence. Officers would show up with light meters in search of deviance in the darkness. Police banned socializing completely: while drinking, customers could not change seats, carry drinks from table to table or even stand up. Drag shows were censored, then banned—and the Garden had to fill in the schedule with girlie shows and brunches. "After 1954, everyone seemed to scatter," said a patron.

In 1956, the City of Seattle significantly increased taxes on bars that served both alcohol and entertainment. The Garden of Allah, unable to afford the increase, quietly closed. It seemed female impersonators had again outworn their welcome, as drag didn't appear again in Seattle for almost six years. Performances, once heavily anchored in talent, became amateur—lip-synching came into fashion, removing any need to sing or dance as drag moved into the gay bars.

THE JEWEL BOX LOUNGE (1948–1982)

An independent Jewel Box operated in Kansas City, Missouri, for nearly four decades. It was known as "the most talked about Night Club in the Midwest" and "Mid-America's Greatest Fun Complex." For years, its one-thousand-seat auditorium was sold out night after night. It's not clear if the club was licensed by Bonner and Brown, but it was absolutely inspired by them.

At age seventy-five, Rae Bourbon (1892–1971) was still the top queen at the Jewel Box. She was famous for releasing a series of "dirty records" popular with the 1950s cocktail set. In December 1968, she made international headlines after being arrested for murder and sentenced to ninety-nine years in prison. She was far, far away from her days of performing for General Franco in Spain, King Edward at Belvedere Castle or at Josephine Baker's Paris Follies. She would never again see Shanghai, Rome or Cairo. The murder trial underscored her long-running issues with the IRS. Rae Bourbon ultimately died while in police custody.

THE BEIGE ROOM (1949–1958)

The Beige Room, "Where Men Are Women," opened as a direct hit on Marge Finocchio. She ruled over San Francisco nightlife with such cruelty, for so long, that the gay community decided to strike back. The Beige Room was a gay-friendly destination that allowed audiences and cast to mingle and socialize, often to the extent of wild afterparties. The Beige Room mocked the tourist trap Finocchio's had become and challenged customers to come see real talent. The Beige Room was the preferred venue for drag performers, who were treated better, paid better and had more control over their stage presence. The Beige closed in 1958 for reasons unknown.

THE DIPLOMAT (c. 1952–1972)

The Diplomat (8540 Second Avenue) was the premier drag theater in Detroit during the 1950s and 1960s. The show ran continuously from 9:30 a.m. to 2:00 a.m. nightly, with a special cocktail hour show Sundays at 5:30 p.m.

Sam "Bookie" Stewart and Morrie Weisberg, the owners of the Diplomat, released an annual review of the drag queens in their show. "Unusual! Sensational! Unique! Exotic!" screamed the ads. "Here at the Club Diplomat, we have what we feel is the most professional and polished group of female impersonators on any stage anywhere today. Your complete entertainment is our reason for being." Vicki Marlane, the world-famous "Lady with the Liquid Spine," was a longtime headliner, as was Rae Bourbon.

Before Stonewall, female impersonators and drag queens came to the Diplomat to find community. Bookie had managed several gay bars and was known to take care of his customers, even bailing them out of jail and sending them coded messages when they were in danger of being entrapped by a vice cop. Like other bars of its era, the Diplomat didn't allow lesbians in male clothing or female impersonators to leave the stage in drag. Oddly, the Michigan Liquor Commission allowed cross-dressers to wear only black shirts and pants for decades.

The Diplomat closed after an electrical fire in 1972, and the Detroit drag scene moved on to the Gold Dollar (3129 Cass Avenue) until it was also destroyed by fire in 2019.

THE BLUE DAHLIA SHOW LOUNGE (1955–1971)

Despite being illegal, drag made a dramatic resurgence in Chicago with the opening of the Blue Dahlia Show Lounge (5640 West North Avenue), billed as "Chicago's Only Female Impersonator Show." Located far outside the city, the Blue Dahlia became an exotic destination for thrill-seekers bored with clean-cut entertainment. Between 1955 and 1971, the Blue Dahlia offered three shows a night (five on Saturdays—the last at 3:45 a.m.) of pantomime, comedy, dancing and "strip artistry." The beautiful neon outside promised "Our Guys Are Dolls." Carefully coordinated payoffs ensured the club's continued success. Caravans of Wisconsin travelers piled into their cars for this exotic, all-night-long experience.

THE JEWEL BOX BEDAZZLES THE WORLD

Bonner and Brown, feeling liberated by their adventurous travels, opened a third Jewel Box Club in Miami in 1946. Rumor has it, they were financed by a wealthy madame with an eye for Brown. Unlike its predecessors, the new Jewel Box was well understood to be a gay bar, with an all-gay staff, but it also became popular with straight crowds.

The earlier Jewel Box Clubs offered live music and heavy pours to a mostly straight audience, but female impersonators were not on the marquee. Florida law prohibited female impersonators to work anywhere that liquor was served. After World War II, this law was somewhat relaxed, and the front bar of the Jewel Box Club was allowed to openly operate as a gay bar.

The shows weren't exactly drawing local audiences, as most of the gay customers found the girls a strange and old-fashioned novelty. The Jewel Box Revue took place in a separate, alcohol-free back room, and the queens were expected to work as B-girls before and after the shows.

"We used to do two-and-a-half-hour shows for four customers," said performer Robin Raye. "The productions were wonderful, but monotonous, and the money wasn't good. They would ask us to go into the front bar, a gay bar, without wigs, and hustle drinks in sweaty makeup and dresses. It was the dumbest thing."

In 1947, the club was raided for having male dancers, which were illegal in Dade County, and for selling alcohol after hours. The club was shut down several times before finally closing permanently in 1952. Since the area was not zoned for a nightclub, and the neighbors protested rezoning, the Jewel Box was demolished for a Jordan Marsh store.

The Jewel Box relocated to the Bal Tabarin nightclub (225 West Forty-Sixth) in Times Square in 1955. By that time, Danny and Doc were world-famous, and the Jewel Box Girls had America eating out of the palm of their hands.

Bonner and Brown were brilliant marketers: after cornering the market on talent, they sought to eliminate any audience suspicion of homosexuality, deviance or deception. Their approach was genius. By introducing performers as men with male pronouns and titles, they set low expectations for an audience that would ultimately be seduced by the onstage illusion. By the end of each show, the audience was convinced these performers were actual women. Even in small-town America, the Jewel Box became the must-see hot ticket show.

For the first time since vaudeville, Jewel Box Revue reintroduced drag as a legitimate and accessible art form. Female impersonation was no longer taboo or controversial. Danny Brown said,

> *The show caught on right from the start, and the reason was that we took the degeneracy out of female impersonation. But during the early part of this century, female impersonation took on an unsavory character and fell out of popularity. We revived the art by staffing our company with actors of unimpeachable moral standards.*
>
> *Our players lead lives that are as normal as any in show business. Nine out of our 30 players are married, and the wife of one of them is our wardrobe mistress. Several of the married men have children and they bring their families along with them when we're on the road. They have no qualms about letting their kids see their act.*
>
> *The Jewel Box Revue is just a clean, family-type show.*

With the Jewel Box Revue, Doc Benner and Danny Brown activated a national queer consciousness. *Wisconsin LGBTQ History Project.*

Together, Bonner and Brown not only created the first gay-positive communities in the country but also seeded the United States with constant queer visibility for three full decades.

Following the sex panic of the late 1930s, the prevailing American mood was that all female impersonators were homosexuals who wanted to be women. Although most believed homosexuality was a disease at the time, there was also a belief that innocents could be seduced or recruited into the lifestyle by gay deceivers. At the earliest Jewel Box performances, theaters hired police and private detectives to ensure patrons didn't touch each other—or the performers—in any way that would be erotic.

As the Jewel Box separated the onstage art form from an offstage transvestite lifestyle, American paranoia quickly disappeared. "The professional impersonator is 99 times out of 100 NOT a homosexual," said a show review. "He may be beautiful and talented, but usually it is just a job he does."

"We appeal to the intellectual who can understand this quirk in a man's nature," said Danny Brown. "There is a bit of woman in every man. For the ones who have an overabundance of female genes, the artists among them take their place in this most entertaining phase of show business. Female impersonation goes back many years in history. It was always considered one of the finer arts of the Romans and Greeks."

"The glamour and mystique of the showgirl," said Doc Benner, "makes this show so appealing."

"You were making fun of yourself, so to speak, so society could accept you," said Jerry Ross. "If you were serious, the public would be offended, so you kept it light."

"I'm not doing this for kicks or to be smart," said Lynne Carter. "It's a way of making a living." Later, the "male Pearl Bailey" would play a solo act at Carnegie Hall on January 20, 1971.

Straight audiences weren't entirely unaware that they were in a genderqueer space, and in retrospect, sexual exploration was probably part of the Jewel Box's appeal. Within the safety of the show experience, curious clubgoers could visit—and even flirt with—a world that they'd never consider outside the cabaret. Knowing, while not knowing, was a sufficient cover story.

As the Jewel Box Girls took the stage, something very unusual happened at the shows. The stars knew how to flirt with the audience, as much as the audience flirted with them. Most of the shows featured heavily homoerotic content that wouldn't be acceptable anywhere else. Knowing the performers were not women, and often pretending to be tricked that they were men, audiences hid behind an imperfect alibi. The Jewel Box offered both a risqué atmosphere—and a safe distance—in which even the most homophobic men could explore a sexual tourism completely free of consequences.

LIFE ON THE ROAD

The Jewel Box shows were absolutely lavish. They truly brought unimaginable glamour to small towns that had never seen anything like it. The opening number, "You Can't Do a Show Without Girls," was their calling card. Lip-synching was strictly not allowed. Early themes ranged from Japanese to Polynesian to Chinese, while later shows featured Carnival in Rio, Arabian Knights, Parisian Can Can, Ziegfeld Follies and even full stage productions. In the 1960s, they added striptease acts. The group was well known for opulent costumes and extravagant sets that rivaled Hollywood or Broadway productions. Headliner Jackie Mayes's wardrobe was insured for $50,000 in the 1950s.

To this day, the Jewel Box staged some of the most extravagant and opulent shows ever performed outside metropolitan cities. They played massive national venues (the Apollo Theater and the Loews State in New York City, the Fox Theater in Detroit, Howard Theater in Washington, D.C., the El Capitan in Los Angeles, Uptown Theater in Philadelphia), the nightclub circuit (Pappy's Showland in Dallas, Café Provincial in Montreal, Roberts

Show Club in Chicago, the Gay 90s in Minneapolis, the Riviera Room in Reno), auditoriums, cocktail lounges, hotel bars and dinner theaters. They appeared in Montreal's Royal Parade on Canada Day and in a Mexican Independence Day celebration in Ciudad Juarez. Because they traveled by road, not air, they never skipped middle America or small towns. Cairo, Illinois, and Flint, Michigan, were frequent stops.

The Jewel Box girls were highly trained, professional performers who were serious about their work. They knew they needed to make as much money as possible to maintain the lifestyle they sought to lead. They relentlessly rehearsed their acts to ensure everything was pinpoint perfect at curtain time.

Audiences noticed. "We got rave reviews from anyone who ever saw us," said Jerry Ross, a longtime performer.

Although souvenir programs still exist from the Jewel Box shows, it doesn't appear a single performance was ever filmed. Rumors abounded for years that a Detroit show was recorded for television, but the footage has never surfaced anywhere.

The Jewel Box inspired numerous copycats, including the Ha Ha Revue, the Powder Puff Revue, the Boody Green Revue, Babe Baker's Revue, the Pearl Box Revue (once headlined by Dorian Corey) and more. Some were more popular than others—but all offered gay and gender nonconforming men a safe sanctuary where they could not only embrace their identities but make a name for themselves.

Bonner and Brown recognized the importance of connecting their show with pop culture, offering lookalikes of Marilyn Monroe, Grace Kelly, Bette Davis, Ava Gardner, Lana Turner and other headliners. The impersonators didn't always hit the mark—and in many cases, they barely tried—but it sure made for a strong marquee.

It wasn't all fun and games. The Detroit police didn't allow them to advertise their shows. In Denver, they were targeted by homophobic ads inviting customers to come see "real girls" like Native Dancer, a local stripper. Some clubs received bomb threats; others were actually bombed, like in Cleveland, where the local Mafia didn't want female impersonators in its clubs. The McCarthy era was terrifying for many Hollywood stars but not the Jewel Box Girls; some of them were dating McCarthy staff members or FBI agents for protection.

Worst of all, the cast was constantly fighting about money.

"The Revue made money, but we never saw much of it," said a former Jewel Boxer. "I liked Doc and Danny, but I feel like they cheated everyone."

CRIMES OF IDENTITY

After a full decade of deliberations, Wisconsin finally joined Michigan and Illinois in implementing a psychopathic offender law in August 1947. The Wisconsin Sex Crimes Law of 1947 allowed police to arrest, detain and institutionalize any sexual "psychopath," regardless of whether the person committed any crime.

What was a sexual psychopath? Anyone with the propensity for murder, rape, exhibitionism, alcoholism, homosexuality or gender confusion. Amazingly, any adult over eighteen could file a statement that someone was a sexual psychopath. The law specifically excused accusers from any liability for damages. It also compelled the local sheriff to investigate and, in most cases, jail the "psychopath." The suspect would be ordered to attend a medical examination, after which they would be committed for "any period of time necessary to affect a cure." If they weren't "cured" or refused to be cured, they could be detained for life.

All it took to destroy a human life forever was one false accusation. Medical journals praised the law as proactive and curative, removing dangerous people from society before they caused damage. Unfortunately, the law was weaponized against homosexual men: 59 percent of arrests were suspected sodomites, whom most lawmakers were eager to "remove" from society.

The Psychopathic Offender Law remained in Wisconsin lawbooks—with some tweaks—until 1980. The timing was especially ironic, however, as the next great drag craze was only a few years away.

THE TIC TOC CLUB

Amid much fanfare, the Jewel Box—with a cast of thirty-five performers—finally made its Milwaukee debut on July 26, 1952, at Albert Tusa's Tic Toc Club (634 North Fifth Street).

"The Tic Toc Club is proud to present Mr. Jackie Mays as the star of the New Jewel Box Revue. Acclaimed by Walter Winchell as the all-time tops in the female impersonator circuit, Jackie is sprinkled with the silver pepper of stardom. His fine performances have caused critics to quip, oh what is so rare as a Jackie Mays," read the event program.

The Tic Toc Club was officially on the national drag circuit. The Jewel Box came back again and again and stayed for ten, twelve, even twenty-five weeks. Milwaukee couldn't get enough of it.

★ ★

The Parade of Stars This Week at the Clubs

═══ NOW PRESENTING ═══

═══ From Miami, Florida ═══

JEWEL BOX REVUE

With 35 of America's Foremost

Femme Mimics

A MUSICAL EXTRAVAGANZA starring

★ MR. JACKIE MAYE ★ MISS MICKEY MERCER, M.C. ★ MR. JACKIE GORDON

"The only girl in the company"

One of the more glittering better-staged and filled with talent groups to come to Milwaukee. Costumed in eye-fascinating manner and on	the show-side, as expert as any you'd see anywhere. It all adds up to something different . . . something that should be on your must list.

FULLY AIR CONDITIONED

TIC TOC CLUB

2 SHOWS NIGHTLY

634 N. 5th St.

Reservations: Phone BR. 2-9270 or 2-9272   8:30 and 11:30

COMPLETE DINNERS *from* **$2.50**

Al Tusa wanted to own a drag cabaret in downtown Milwaukee. He almost got his wish. *Milwaukee Public Library.*

Notorious bootlegger Albert Tusa opened the Tic Toc on July 25, 1940, promising the "finest in entertainment every night." For years, the Tic Toc competed against Liberace, who was playing piano at the nearby Red Room.

Tusa was known as the "Milwaukee guy who pays the big salaries," because he brought in national talent that (somehow) rarely turned a profit. In fact, most stars were booked at a loss to the club simply to bring them to Milwaukee. He carried himself with big-city swagger, carrying a solid gold cigarette case and serving only the highest of top-shelf liquors. With the tagline "It's Always Cool," the Tic Toc Club was one of the first air-conditioned nightclubs in Milwaukee (and famously refused to turn it off during wartime rations). His "cool factor" caught the eye of national magazines: the Tic Toc was named one of America's top ten dinner theaters from 1948 to 1953.

Billboard and *Variety* regularly reported on the Tic Toc Club's lineup, which featured some of the biggest names of the era. Tusa developed friendships with Martha Raye, Sophie Tucker, Eddie Cantor, Jimmy Durante, Joey

Bishop and other Hollywood names, usually inviting them to his home for a family dinner while they were in town. Unable to meet the salary demands of one famous chanteuse's agent, he called her directly and talked her into lowering her price. "I'll come only on one condition," she said, "you need to make your famous spaghetti with lobster sauce." (The chanteuse was reportedly Josephine Baker.)

Underneath that good-old-boy exterior, Tusa dabbled with the dark side. Al Tusa had legal and financial trouble dating back to the 1920s that haunted his entire career. Despite his best efforts to turn the Tic Toc into the Milwaukee version of Finocchio's or the Garden of Allah, he just could not secure the local funding (or the local talent) to open his own drag cabaret.

With new emcee Stormé DeLarverie as the "one girl," the Jewel Box came back to Milwaukee on May 27, 1955. The troupe had been booked for the Tic Toc, but the Tic Toc was gone—the victim of Tusa's overindulgence—so the Jewel Box played at the less-popular Club 26 (2601 West North Avenue). Tusa moved on to operate the Pink Pony, a high-end cocktail lounge at 1834 West North Avenue.

The Jewel Box returned to Milwaukee on May 17, 1959, for a three-week engagement at the Brass Rail (774 North Third Street). Jim Koconis, Milwaukee's "Night Life Chatter" columnist, offered a review of opening night: "They've been featured in many of the better nighteries from Hollywood to Miami. The revue features a colorful display of song, dance, and comedy skits, as presented by the world's greatest femme impersonators. What slayed me was the brush haircut on the tuxedo-clad boy emcee, who is a girl, among so many long-haired boys who are, aw heck, you figure it out."

Only three years old, the Brass Rail was a reputable jazz club. Three days after the Jewel Box's May 31, 1959 departure, the Brass Rail changed format permanently. "Management is considering a change in policy," reported Koconis on May 30, 1959, "and it's looking like girlie shows." After being forcibly acquired by the Balistrieri crime family, the Brass Rail became a notorious striptease joint for the next twenty-five years.

It wouldn't be the last time the Jewel Box inspired the Balistrieris.

ADRIAN AMES

Adrian Ames, the self-proclaimed "Million Dollar Drag Queen," "The Floor Show Unto Himself," "The Town's Most Scintillating Star" and "Milwaukee's

Nobody could promote Adrian Ames better than Adrian Ames himself. *Milwaukee Public Library.*

Favorite Female Impersonator," made his local debut on December 5, 1949, with a $10,000 movieland wardrobe of gowns, furs and jewels. Earl Carroll described him as "the most beautiful boy in women's clothes." His ads said, "The Name Adrian Ames Means Business," and he absolutely meant it. No one was ever quite sure where Adrian Ames came from—he just seemed to explode on the scene, and he was the talk of the town.

"Emcee Jimmy Method is adding a major attraction tonight," said the *Milwaukee Journal.* "Mr. Adrian Ames, Hollywood's Favorite Female Impersonator, who has been so sensational in Chicago, New York, San Francisco and Palm Beach, opens tonight at Club Terris. Many have copied our shows—none have equaled. Egypt had Cleopatra—Club Terris now has Adrian Ames."

Soon, Adrian Ames was selling out crowds for months on end—and Jimmy Method was off the marquee entirely. "Mix and mingle with famous faces every night," said the ads, "as we bring Paris to Milwaukee."

Buck Herzog of the *Milwaukee Sentinel* reported, "With the passing of Julian Eltinge, it was said in show circles that the days of the plush female impersonator were gone. Judging by the crowds which have packed Tommy

Terris' Theatrical Club, where Adrian Ames has been performing the past eight weeks, this facet of show business has sprung to renewed life."

Ames explained,

> *This has been my work for 20 years. I started in show business as a dramatic actor, but when a role came up to impersonate a woman I was selected. I did so well—and really liked it—that I continued the impersonation. It has been quite lucrative, too....*
>
> *They look, and they touch me, Sure, I'm padded in some places, but fashion creators have told me that I have a figure most models would envy. How did I get it? Well, nature does those things. Impersonating a woman takes a lot of study and rehearsal for a guy like me who likes football and a good drink of bourbon. It's a darn good business and I like it.*

Herzog, perhaps inspired by manly mentions of sports and liquor, asked Ames if he planned to marry. He replied, "Are you kidding? It's what everybody hopes for, man or woman," before taking out his pipe, puffing profusely and barking out, "I'm breaking in a new girdle tonight and it's killing me."

Ames performed at Club Terris for forty straight weeks before moving to Club Milwaukeean in September 1950. "This fabulous act is a must-see for all who enjoy something new, unique and definitely different in the way of top entertainment," said columnist Jim Koconis on March 14, 1953.

At the height of McCarthy-era homosexual panic, Adrian Ames—an out gay man and female impersonator—ruled Milwaukee nightlife, fashion and gossip columns with a well-manicured iron fist.

Milwaukee had never seen anything like Adrian Ames. If he wasn't in the society pages, he found ways to create mentions for himself. "He has the only mink cape stole in all of Milwaukee, and it's sapphire blue. Say boy!" wrote a local fashion columnist on April 26, 1950. "Adrian Ames opens Monday at the Club Milwaukeean with a Russian Wolf Hound added to his wardrobe," said another on September 12, 1950. "If you're interested in purchasing a French poodle, contact Adrian Ames, now performing at Lakota's," read a March 1956 press release. "The poodle, who goes by the name Lilly, tore Ames' 12-dollar hat to shreds the other day. So now, it must go!"

He was explosive, colorful, flamboyant and fabulous—not just onstage, but in everyday life. For these reasons, his name immediately became synonymous with gay. Jim Koconis, in his June 27, 1950 column, warned theatergoers that Senorita Herrero was an "Adrian Ames type" and that guys should "get wise!"

Adrian Ames ruled Milwaukee nightlife for over a decade. *Wisconsin LGBTQ History Project.*

Ames and the Milwaukee media certainly had a love-hate relationship. "I ran into Adrian Ames at Club Terris," wrote Jim Koconis in a November 13, 1954 article, "and he said, 'listen you, stop using my material on these second-rate acts around town.' He was referring to some adjectives that performers liked to slap in front of their stage names. I told him from now on, I would check with Webster's Dictionary to be sure the words had clear title."

Club Milwaukeean lost its license in 1957 after receiving eighty violations. It reopened as Club Jay-Jay, which focused on African American dance music. Adrian Ames moved to Club 26, where he performed seven nights a week for two years.

By September 1959, Ames was bored with Milwaukee and bound for bigger things. "After a big, big, big run on the coast, this town is dead. If I could sell my property here, I would leave town, and I mean it," he told the *Journal*. The *Journal* responded, "OK real estate men, that's your cue."

After touring both coasts, Adrian Ames decided it was time to leave Milwaukee for good, but he wasn't leaving without a grand finale. He recruited performers from both Club 82 and Finocchio's to spend the summer in Milwaukee, performing four shows a week on the stage where he earned his fame twelve years earlier.

On May 10, 1961, his *Paris to Harlem Revue* opened for a twelve-week run at Club Jay-Jay. Despite a massive ad campaign, personally hand-designed by Ames himself, the somewhat out-of-date show was later seen as a commercial flop. Club Jay-Jay was demolished later that year for the construction of I-43 and the Hillside Interchange.

Determined to make a profit, Ames ran the show for twelve full weeks. But Milwaukee's decade-long drag craze had already come to an end, leaving Ames with a half-empty house and an empty bank account. All the great drag cabarets of the 1950s had already closed, and drag was now found only in the city's emerging gay bars.

Ames moved to San Francisco, where he continued to perform at Finocchio's and other venues throughout the 1970s. He died in October 1980 of natural causes.

The *San Francisco Crusader* planned a memorial issue in Ames's honor, but it never happened. It seems nobody could "do" Adrian Ames like Adrian Ames himself.

BILLIE HERRERO

Abandoned by his unwed mother, Billy overcame an orphanage childhood to tour the world as one of the first international drag superstars. As a nine-year-old child living in Los Angeles, Herrero was inspired by the farewell performance of Julian Eltinge, the wealthiest female impersonator of the vaudeville era.

"I saw this fat old man in women's clothing, and I thought to myself, whatever he can do, I can do better," he told interviewers. He claimed to have been trained in dance, dress and "womanhood" by Rita Hayworth herself.

Herrero was only fifteen when he started performing in the Third Ward's cut-rate cabarets. It's unclear what brought him to Milwaukee, but it seems he made his drag debut here. He was known for his Dolores Del Rio, Hedy Lamarr and Pola Negri acts. When cross-dressing was criminalized, Billy moved to San Francisco to perform at Finocchio's.

Twelve years later, Billie Herrero returned to Milwaukee to steal the spotlight. His rendition of Gypsy Rose Lee was so perfect that audiences thought they were watching the real actress. In fact, Gypsy's former nanny traveled to Milwaukee to see the show—and left believing that Gypsy Rose Lee had been a man all along.

Billie Herrero was nationally famous as the "Brazilian Gypsy Rose Lee." *Wisconsin LGBTQ History Project.*

By 1950, Billie was making over $3,000 per week in downtown Milwaukee. "Billie Herrero made over a million dollars in her day," he said later, "but she spent it all on luxuries."

Then he made a huge mistake: on a dare, he invited the real Gypsy Rose Lee to come see him, thinking she would be flattered. "I won't have it," she declared from her front-row seat, two minutes into the show. "How dare you? I'll sue you." Her lawyers backed up the threat. "A cheaper version of Gypsy Rose Lee threatens her livelihood," they argued. (The opposite was true: clubs that sold out for Billie Herrero saw smaller crowds when they booked the real Gypsy Rose Lee.) With nine weeks left in her contract, Billie was terminated on October 25, 1950, due to the "Gypsy Heat." It seems her last show was at Club 26 (2601 West North Avenue) on New Year's Eve 1953.

By 1954, Herrero was broke and fed up with nightlife. He retired from entertainment, went back to being "Billy" and relocated to Florida. Rich with clutter, he operated an antiques shop in Coconut Grove for many years.

Old age was not kind to the former sensation. Deeply depressed, going blind, facing eviction and over $500,000 in debt, Billy set his home on fire and died by suicide on Christmas Eve 1992. A large coffee table book, titled *How to Live a Victorious Life*, was one of the only survivors of the fire. His collection of show business memorabilia, dating back six decades, was sold at auction.

There was no memorial service for Billy. He had few friends and no surviving family. Untrusting of the world since childhood, he had never allowed himself to be romantic. Most of his co-workers and fans had already passed away.

"I've enjoyed the company of dignitaries and degenerates," he told a Miami magazine shortly before his suicide. "I have had an amazing life."

A STORMÉ LIFE

> *When you grew up like me, honey, you better be able to see all the way around you, because when the black kids weren't chasing me, the white kids were chasing me, and if they weren't, the dogs were chasing me, or the snakes were chasing me. Somebody was always chasing me—until I stopped running.*
>
> *—Stormé DeLarverie*

Stormé DeLarverie (1920–2014), the "one girl" of the Revue, joined in 1955. She was visiting Miami and learned that Brown and Brenner needed help with their show. Micky Mercer, the original "1 Girl" of the cast, had gone solo, and they needed a host. Stormé planned to stay for only six months, but that six months turned into fourteen years. She became the host, musical director and stage manager over time. In her senior years, DeLarverie recalled her days with the Jewel Box Revue as the best of her life, although she felt the troupe never received proper recognition for being the forerunner it was in the 1950s and 1960s.

Stormé was unique—especially among the gender-focused Jewel Box cast—as she defied any definition of gender identity both onstage and offstage. As a teenager, Stormé ran away to ride horses for the Ringling Brothers Circus. She began singing as a woman and then began presenting as a man as an early adult. Her baritone voice earned her a jazz tour of Europe. Later, she was a bodyguard for Chicago mobsters who never suspected she was not a man.

"You wear men's clothing, but you don't want to hurt a man's feelings, because you are really a woman in his shoes," said Stormé, who always sought to deliver a tasteful act.

"It was very easy. All I had to do was just be me and let people use their imaginations," she said in *Stormé: The Lady of the Jewel Box*. "It never changed me. I was still a woman."

Audiences spent most of the show trying to guess who the "one girl" was. Little did they know that it was their swarthy host and emcee. In a closing number, Stormé removed her mustache and her tailored jacket to reveal herself with "A Surprise with a Song." The Jewel Box was so influential on queer culture that 1950s lesbian fashion mimicked Stormé's masculine look for decades. She became an unlikely celebrity, hobnobbing with Dinah Washington, Billie Holiday, Ella Fitzgerald, Nina Simone and other prominent African American artists of the time. She carried on a long-term romance with Diana, a dancer she met in New York City. In 1961, she was photographed by Diane Arbus in the famous "Miss Stormé DeLarverie, the Lady Who Appears to Be a Gentleman, N.Y.C."

"She lived on both sides of the coin," said friend Lisa Cannistraci. "She refused to choose. She didn't live as a man or a woman. She lived a Stormé life, and I loved that about her."

On June 27, 1969, Stormé found herself at the historic Stonewall Uprising. There's still some debate about whether she was the "New York City butch" who instigated the riot. Later, witnesses would recall a "dyke-stone butch" throwing a punch at a menacing police officer, evading arrest multiple times, fighting multiple officers and beckoning to white male crowds to "do something." Many consider that woman the "Rosa Parks of the gay rights movement—and Stormé always told friends that was her."

"A cop said to me, 'Move along, faggot!' thinking I was a gay guy. I said, 'I will not. And don't you dare touch me,'" said DeLarverie. "The cop shoved me, and I instinctively punched him right in the face. The cops hit me, and I hit him back. The cops got what they gave." Miss Major, also present at the Uprising, spit in the face of a police officer, was knocked unconscious and awoke in a jail cell.

Stormé DeLarverie was the "1 Girl" of the Jewel Box Revue for fifteen years. *Wisconsin LGBTQ History Project.*

Stormé left the Jewel Box on September 7, 1969. She moved into the Chelsea Hotel and served as a bodyguard for wealthy New York families, a bouncer for lesbian bars in the West Village and an unlikely pistol-packing street vigilante. Stormé declared herself a "babysitter of my people, all my boys and girls," and roamed the West Village in search of anyone hassling or harassing the "baby girls" of the bar scene.

"She literally walked the streets of downtown Manhattan like a gay superhero," said Cannistraci, owner of the Cubbyhole women's bar. "She was not to be messed with."

"She was the sweetest gun-toting octogenarian you could ever meet," said a friend. "She was the most effective bouncer in the business. It was impossible not to like her."

Even into her eighties, Stormé was a board member of the Stonewall Veterans Association and a regular New York Pride Parade honoree. She would occasionally sing at charity events and fundraisers, supporting victims of domestic and childhood abuse.

"I'm a human being that survived. So, I helped other people survive," she told documentarians in 2001.

She passed away in her sleep on May 24, 2014, in New York City. Five years later, she was one of the first fifty honorees on the National LGBTQ Wall of Honor at the Stonewall National Monument, the first U.S. national monument dedicated to LGBTQ history.

MIDCENTURY MILWAUKEE'S DRAG CRAZE

Thanks to these iconic headliners, drag was back. And in many ways, it was more mainstream than ever before:

- World-famous Mr. Paris Delair joined Lucian, the male Sophie Tucker; Mr. Mademoiselle Maurice, Teenia Deaquina; and Valda Gray as the headliners of The Flame (1315 North Ninth Street).
- Lee Rainor's Satin and Sequin Revue, featuring Carol Cramer and five other girls, headlined Club Ron-De-Voo (1126 West North Avenue).
- Lee Wong the China Doll ran the house at Club 26.
- The Exotic and Loveable Tarza was the star of Floyd's Black & Tan (1222 North Seventh Street).
- Guilda of Paris and Fatima the Harem Dancer were the stars of Lakota's (602 West Wisconsin).

Within a year or two, drag shows were also happening at The Gay 90s (756 North Plankinton Avenue) and the Crystal Palace (402 North Water

Street), old-school taverns that were borderline gay bars while offering luncheon shows to women's and senior groups from the Jewish Community Center. Henri's Show Lounge (730 North Fifth Street), the Lampost Bar (440 West Michigan Street) and Rancho's Club (1665 North Third Street) started showing "he/she shows."

Even the dusty old Empress Burlesk House (755 North Third Street) jumped on the bandwagon, replacing its all-girl cast with a fleet of far-cheaper female impersonators. The only difference was that the Empress couldn't afford big-name girls or traveling troupes. Jim Koconis, nightlife reporter, said, "A glimpse of stocking used to be quite shocking at the Empress in dad's day, but nowadays, you'll be more shocked at what passes for a broad!" Bunny might have said it best: "Where drag queens went to die. Those girls weren't even trying anymore." It wouldn't be the first time that drag shows were on the marquee, but it would be the last. The Empress switched from fourth-rate drag to fourth-run movies in early 1951.

Drag was so popular in the city that the Dave Miller Costume Shop (919 North Jackson) was exclusively serving the impersonator community. Most surprisingly, the *Milwaukee Sentinel* began to run want ads in November 1954 for amateur female impersonators seeking others in the community.

Even Club La Tosca (now at 631 East Clybourn Street) was still running midnight shows—until a February 6, 1955 after-hours raid finally shut it down.

Of all the venues, Club Terris was perhaps the most surprising of them all. Owned by Tom Terris, boxing promoter and businessman, Club Terris had "the world's longest bar" (at three hundred feet) surrounding a boxing ring. The club was known for wrestling, boxing and sports shows—and then it jumped into the drag ring throughout the 1950s. Club Terris burned badly in 1960 and was demolished in 1964. (Tom Terris went on to open the Riverboat Restaurant on Commerce Street.)

It's important to understand that none of these venues could fairly be called a gay bar, at least, not yet. In 1950s Milwaukee, drag was happening only in straight nightclubs for entertainment, mostly forbidden in the city's early gay bars.

As a pre–Civil War warehouse district, the Plankinton Strip (400 block North) wasn't ever a very pretty part of town. It was Milwaukee's twentieth-century Tenderloin—at least, while it lasted. Most buildings were covered with eighty years of coal soot, making it seem much older and dirtier than it was. While property owners deferred postwar maintenance and waited for their condemnation orders, it got less pretty every day. Knowing that a freeway was coming, most businesses moved out during World War II, including an entire agricultural seed industry that vanished overnight. The Plankinton Strip quickly became an in-between place that people drove through to go somewhere else. Since nobody really lived here, the only people who came here were "insiders" looking for places that didn't want to be known or found by outsiders.

The Strip included the Fox Bar (455 North Plankinton, opened 1948), the Old Mill Inn (400 North Plankinton, 1933–1959) and the old sailor bar Anchor Inn (401 North Plankinton, 1933–1949). Other known gay landmarks included the Mint Bar (422 West Wells, opened 1949), the Clifton Tap (336 West Juneau Avenue), Sallys (741 North Fourth Street), the Antlers Hotel Mural Bar (616 North Second Street), the White Horse (1426 North Eleventh Street), the Seaway Inn (744 North Jefferson Street) and the aforementioned Red Room and Royal Hotel Bars. None of these bars dared to serve people in drag—except at the Mint Bar, originally limited to a New Year's or Halloween costume. Female impersonators made cash-paying customers uncomfortable, as they usually attracted and expected attention. As a result, they were rarely allowed in Milwaukee gay bars before the mid-1960s. The one rather unusual exception was the Wildwood (1430 West Walnut Street), a butch lesbian hangout from 1949 to 1963, which allowed "queens" in its later years but still never allowed men.

After fifteen years in business, the Tic Toc Club was sold at auction on Tuesday, March 30, 1955, to Harry Kaminsky and the Auto Acceptance Corporation for $14,000. From the outside in, Kaminsky viewed the Tic Toc as a highly profitable venture, especially since it welcomed homosexuals who had few other places to go. While he toyed with the idea of opening his first gay bar here, the timing—and the location—just weren't right for 1955. The business was bought by the Fazio brothers and became the famous Fazio's on Fifth. It was the end of an era and the end of female impersonator shows at 634 North Fifth Street, at least for a while.

Where did they all go? A 1958 arrest offers one hint: police raided and closed an underground drag club at 2145 North Palmer Street, where two "known female impersonators" had converted a flat into a performance venue. The fourteen-officer raid arrested eleven "inmates" for suspected prostitution.

THE VELVET CAGE

Bonner and Brown knew how to position themselves—and their artists—in a straight business world that rarely understood what they were working with. They knew that their shows catered to a gay audience but earned mainstream acceptance from straight audiences to create access and equity for their performers. They were overprotective—even maternal—in their approach to the "family."

They paid living wages and medical expenses, provided insurance for their performers' wardrobes and always ensured everyone was well fed. They were fiercely protective of that family and never afraid to fight anyone who would dare harass, abuse or discriminate against their "children." Hecklers often learned a hard lesson.

The Jewel Box girls were considered valuable and collectable assets and were closely protected against violence, harassment and discrimination while part of the troupe.

Staffed exclusively by gay men (and later, one lesbian), the Jewel Box Revue was a remarkable midcentury refuge for gay performers. However, this arrangement didn't guarantee the artists any sort of authentic or honest life offstage. In many ways, the Jewel Box girls were neutered. They lived a sheltered, lonely and loveless life. They spoke of wives, girlfriends and other manly love interests to their audiences and reporters, but these were only deliberate cover stories to maintain their reputation as "boy-a-logical experts."

Life in the Jewel Box was very limiting for gay men, no matter how liberating their onstage performances seemed. They were celebrities as long as they never left the stage. Benner and Brown didn't allow dating within the troupe, as they didn't want to deal with any drama. Performers weren't allowed to date the audience, either, as it might invite prostitution charges. While visiting gay bars on their own, the Jewel Box Girls faced criticism and contempt from gay men who felt they were perpetuating outdated stereotypes at the community's expense.

"'What's the matter honey,' they'd ask us," said a performer in 1980. "'You can't find a real man? You have to go out at night with your sisters?' People could be so mean."

The Jewel Box Girls were trapped in the closet as long as they were in the show. Police were raiding gay bars and brutalizing homosexuals even as the Jewel Box was performing sold-out full-capacity drag shows nearby. Bonner and Brown were also trapped in this velvet cage. Although openly gay, they

The Tic Toc Club (1940–1955) was a frequent stop for the Jewel Box Revue. *Wisconsin LGBTQ History Project.*

could not be flamboyant or openly affectionate, and they never spoke of their sexual identities in public.

By 1962, female impersonation hit an all-time high in popularity. The Jewel Box Girls were asked to appear on radio and TV talk shows about beauty tips. They were showcased as superwomen in national magazines. Even the New York Rockettes brought their beauty problems to the Jewel Box Revue. They became an inspiration for not only drag queens but also bored housewives.

The Jewel Box Girls inspired several mail-order magazines, including *Female Mimics* and *Him-Her*. The magazines often featured testimonials from straight, married men who could no longer deny their female identities. Most writers included amateur snapshots of themselves to complement the more fashionable photoplays. "Some of our readers are more masculine than the rugged he-man you see in movies," said *Female Mimics*.

These magazines were important in mobilizing the growing trans community. As a 1966 letter to *He-She* read, "I admire your courage in presenting the case for the transvestite to the general public. There are for more of us than is generally realized, but many of us don't realize there are others with the same taste for changing roles. To know we are NOT alone is to improve our general outlook."

But fame was fleeting. By the late 1960s, Black activists had turned against the Jewel Box Revue, stating that female impersonators threatened the Black family by confusing Black male gender roles. On December 4, 1969, the widely publicized thirtieth anniversary show at Harlem's historic Apollo Theater was boycotted and picketed. "The dregs and drags of society are polluting our community," read a flyer. "Keep the Queers out of Harlem."

The Jewel Box kept pushing onward, but it was well past its prime. It was described as an "all-drag Lawrence Welk show," "out of date with the 1970s."

"[Female impersonators] were just so square back then," said filmmaker and author John Waters in a 2016 interview. "They wanted to be real women, Miss America, maybe their mother? They were straight out of that movie, 'The Queen.' They took things so seriously that they couldn't even laugh at themselves. Divine didn't want to be a woman. She wanted to be Godzilla. She wanted nothing to do with pageants."

After a final show at New York's Bijou Theater in 1975, the Jewel Box was retired forever. Benner and Brown moved to Hallandale, where they died months apart in 1976. "They took show business for a Boy-Ride!" read the papers.

BUNNY OPPER (1936–2020)

Spirited, sassy, carefree and colorful, "Bunny" began his life as George Opper in rural Grafton, Wisconsin, on April 21, 1936. Bored with the country life, the thrill-seeking teen hitchhiked his way downtown as early as age thirteen. For Bunny, midcentury Milwaukee was a playground. Long before dating apps existed, he would meet like-minded friends at the Greyhound Bus Station or Milwaukee Road Station. "You'd wait, you'd watch, and you'd follow them out. That's how I found the men and the bars."

"We'd get together, dress up in drag and ride the bus around Milwaukee with our cocktails," said Bunny. "Just for fun!"

Bunny said the longest relationship of his life was with the Mint Bar (422 West Wells Street), which opened in 1949, relocated in 1986 and closed in 1992. The little twelve-stool tavern hosted a chosen family, including owners

Bettie and Angelo Aiello, staff Rosie and Tracy and longtime friends from all walks of life.

"Everyone used to go all out on New Year's Eve at the Mint Bar, because it was their anniversary night. It was a black tie, white glove, plan your drag outfit for weeks in advance event. We'd stay there all night until Annadel's [diner] opened up and pray to hell we didn't pass out at the counter in last night's drag."

Bunny always lamented the loss of the original "Fruit Loop," starting with the six-alarm arson destruction of Tony's Riviera (401 North Plankinton Avenue) in March 1964. "I was in California and got a call: 'your house is on fire, come home right away!'" When he got home, the bar was gone.

"People always told me; you are crazy to go out in drag. You're going to get beat up, or worse yet, kidnapped and murdered," said Bunny. "But to be honest, I never worried about it. I once sauntered into the Belmont Hotel Coffee Shop totally nude at three o'clock in the morning, my mink stole dragging behind me. No one blinked."

"Only once did someone call me a faggot on the street. I told him you're right, mister, but you just met a faggot who knows how to fight. And I showed him how faggots fight back. Nobody ever called me names again after that!"

Police persecution was a real danger for Bunny's generation, especially once Judge Christ T. Seraphim vowed to liberate Milwaukee from homosexuals in 1963. Many experienced harassment, intimidation and violence. Careers, marriages, families and reputations were not the only casualties in the "war against perversion." Suicides were a common—and commonly underreported—reaction to being exposed. As the pressure to fill arrest quotas accelerated, the "war on perversion" started to have a body count.

Elroy Schulz, brewery worker, was arrested in Juneau Park in April 1960 after supposedly grabbing a vice officer and making an "immoral proposition." In the process of being arrested, Elroy suffered shattered dentures, diabetic shock, abdominal bleeding and a brain hemorrhage. The officer claimed to have hit him only once.

Schulz died before sunrise, less than five hours after his discharge. His killers were cleared of charges of excessive force. "The officer acted justifiably and excusably in the due process of the law and could not be held criminally responsible," reads the inquest. "No charges will be filed."

"People can't understand a problem they don't see. We see them—these men are predatory. They hang around theaters, stores, and public restrooms. They are a threat to public decency," explained a veteran police officer.

George "Bunny" Opper tested all the limits of midcentury Milwaukee. *Wisconsin LGBTQ History Project.*

Elroy Schulz's death was a chilling reminder that gay people could expect no mercy.

"For most of the hidden homosexuals, it is a furtive, lonely life of passing attachments, a life haunted by fear of exposure, loss of job, blackmail and perhaps guilt. It is gay only in homosexual jargon," reads a 1960 *Milwaukee Sentinel* article.

But a great awakening was already happening in Milwaukee. An emerging generation was not afraid to step out of the shadows to fight in the sunlight. "If we were going to hell anyway," said Bunny, "we were going to hell in high heels."

4

LIBERATION (1961–1980)

We do not run from a fight. We do not run from anything.

Inspired by the drag craze of the 1950s and early 1960s and the stars of stage, screen and television, a new generation began to push the limits of acceptability. Cross-dressing on stage had become cross-dressing in real life: no longer limited by their performance personas, young urban "queens" began to present and express themselves as female in their everyday social lives.

In response to this unusual movement, police in Chicago and Milwaukee began to cite the "three-article rule," which dictated that all people had to be wearing three articles of gendered clothing in public. Violators could be apprehended, publicly inspected and even arrested. There was no unisex clothing at the time: either you were dressed as a boy or you were dressed as a girl. And that was up to the police to decide.

The "queens" were born too late: the national drag circuit had essentially collapsed, female impersonators no longer held exclusive nightclub residencies and traveling troupes like the Jewel Box Revue would soon be seen as uncool and old-fashioned. So, they chose to push the limits, break the rules and create a whole new society for themselves.

They might never get rich, but by damned, they were going to be famous.

JAIME HERNANDEZ, AKA JAMIE GAYS (1946–)

Jamie Gays won many titles, including Miss Gay Milwaukee, throughout his long career. *Wisconsin LGBTQ History Project.*

Jamie Hernandez graduated from South Division High School in 1964. Jamie chose to live an openly gay life, which meant enduring social stigma, harassment and gay bashing, often from people who sought his sexual attention. Although cross-dressing was illegal in Milwaukee, Jamie went out in full drag on a regular basis.

Jamie was the club kid of his time. He made things happen simply by showing up. "They weren't part of the scene, they were the scene," Wisconsin LGBTQ History Project contributors have said about Jamie Gays and his friend Josie Carter. He became famous for his rendition of Donna Summer's "Last Dance." He won Miss Castaways 1969, Miss Gay Milwaukee 1971, Miss Factory 1973, Miss Gay Wisconsin 1976 and many, many more competitions. Along the way, Jamie inspired a Milwaukee drag tradition that continues to thrive today.

"I never wanted to compete, but my husbands made me," Jamie said in 2011. "And the whole time, my mother made my gowns."

"I've been called feminine all my life, but a lot of people took the hormones to be feminine," said Jamie. "You would hear about a doctor so-and-so, but it wasn't like you got a prescription, or even an appointment. There was just this big bag of pills."

One time, I went to Chicago, because all these girls were getting these big tits and everything, and I wanted to see how they were getting them. And I'm looking at this doctor, if he was even a doctor, in this dirty hotel room, and he was injecting these girls we knew, all in a row.

I'm watching this, and I'm asking myself, what the hell is going on. This doctor injects one in there, and one in there, and did not even change the needle, and goes on to a third person. I said "No, you're not touching me." Good thing too.

One girl got her shots—and her tits went all black. Another one lost her breasts, they took off and ran down into her arms, and she had to go have it scraped out and done all over again. Another one's hips fell to her ankles. You've never seen anything like it. They said it was chicken fat. It was black as tar, and they injected it here and there and everywhere.

They charged $1,800. Where did these girls even get that kind of money? They had no money. People started getting sick from these. I'm sure some people died. You think anything happened to those doctors? I'm not talking about one hundred years ago; this was the 1970s. This is the price we paid to be beautiful.

A proud Puerto Rican, Jamie understood the social pressures felt by Latinx LGBTQ youth. In 2009, Jamie was honored at PrideFest Milwaukee for his leadership role in the Hispanic community. Today, Jamie is retired and living in Milwaukee.

JOSIE CARTER (c.1941–2014)

By the age of five, "Joseph" knew something wasn't right. He just wasn't interested in "boy" things, no matter how hard he tried. In early puberty, Joseph survived a sexual assault by an older white man. This triggered not only a mistrust of men—white men in particular—but also an exploration of who he really was.

Was I born in the wrong body? These thoughts flooded Joseph's mind night and day. Finally, he started expressing the person he felt he was inside. His mother "made no mind of it"; maybe this was just a little rebellion. It didn't matter either way; she loved her child no matter what. And that's how "Josie" was born, right before age fifteen.

"You have to understand," said Josie. "It was really hard to shop for women's clothes in the 50s and 60s. The department stores just did not allow it. You start looking around any dress shop and be damned if some uptight white woman was not right there on you with her clipboard asking you why. They would ask you to leave the store even if they just suspected you were a queen."

They wouldn't even sell nylons or fingernail polish to men back then. Not even hair coloring. Lots of girls had to shoplift cosmetics. It was the only way to get them. I do not joke. The one and only way. "I'm buying these for my girlfriend" did not cut it week after week. Salespeople watched, they kept track, they noticed everything. They were so worried about keeping things separated.

More of a nightlife personality than a performer, Josie Carter was the "It Girl" of the 1960s. *Wisconsin LGBTQ History Project.*

People would dare me to try on these expensive gowns at the department stores. Jamie would do that because she is crazy, and she could get away with it. And she could run faster than me! So that left two choices: shop the secondhand stores or make your own clothes. I was not about to go out wearing some dead woman clothes, so I got good at dressing myself. I learned fast; it is really easy to look like a million bucks.

"I started going out in drag when I was eighteen," said Josie. "My first gay bar was the White Horse, because I knew Black folk could go in there. The gay life was taboo at that time, period. All the bars were dark, no lights nowhere. Most gay people didn't want to be seen, but I wanted people to see me. I felt like the gay bars were the first place I ever was really seen."

"The owners of the bars always had a thing for me," Josie added.

People watched out for me so nobody would take advantage of me. Bar owners were paying off the crooked cops to look the other way. There was a lot of under the table stuff. And I do mean a lot! I knew a lot of cops and they taught me how things worked. They'd walk into the bar, go into the back room, they'd get themselves some drinks, some cigars and some fat envelopes, and they'd leave. The next night, they might call the bars and say, you're going to get raided tonight. Everyone with something to worry about would know to stay home. So yeah, they'd protect us.

The gays made some police officers rich. So, no, I didn't really get harassed by cops. Who would dare to harass us? The police needed us to keep on coming and spending our money, or there would be no money to pay them. Nobody was going to lay a hand on us, unless they wanted that hand shot right off.

Josie wouldn't be pushed around, not if she could help it. If you were aggressive toward her, she would put you in your place. Over the years, she earned the title "Mother of Gay Milwaukee" for housing, feeding and caring for gay youth whose own mothers had rejected and abandoned them.

Josie saw the world while serving her country as a steward's maid in the U.S. Navy. She toured Hawaii, Japan, Fiji, New Zealand and the South Pacific. After an honorable discharge, Josie entered the workforce on her own terms. Employment was difficult at first, especially for an androgynous

Josie, the "Mother of Gay Milwaukee," was a loyal friend and caregiver to many. *Wisconsin LGBTQ History Project.*

Black man. She accepted whatever jobs would pay the bills, which led her to a foreman career at Capitol Stamping.

Her natural family began after one night with a lady friend. "All it takes is once," Josie said, "and that is so true." Nine months later, her son Larry Joe was born. When Larry Joe was three years old, she appealed to the judge for full custody—and won.

Although she dressed, expressed and presented in female identity, Josie described herself "more of a personality than a performer." She did drag shows in the 1960s and early 1970s, including a famous "African Voodoo" fire dance at the Fox Bar, until her husband asked her to stop performing. After that, she only did numbers on special requests, such as friends' anniversary or birthday parties.

THE BLACK NITE CHANGES EVERYTHING

Eight years before Stonewall, Milwaukee was the scene of an early uprising unlike anything local police had ever seen before. On Saturday night, August 5, 1961, four troublemakers got more trouble than they bargained for at the Black Nite (400 North Plankinton Avenue), one of Milwaukee's most popular gay bars of the time.

Long known as the Old Mill Tavern and Cafe, the ground-floor storefront was acquired by local financier Harry Kaminsky in 1959. Unable to get a tavern license in his name, Kaminsky convinced Mary Wathen of Omaha, Nebraska, to operate the tavern for one year. In exchange, he would pay for her son's tuition at St. John's Academy.

Mary complained immediately about being "bothered" by homosexual clientele from nearby taverns. "They drove regular customers away," she complained to Kaminsky, whose response was, "If we can't beat 'em, let's join 'em."

Kaminsky was on to something. The Plankinton Strip had been the gay go-to since the Great Depression, and the short-lived Pink Glove (631 North Broadway) proved there was big money to be made in gay bars. So, Mary's Tavern joined the block.

Mary's was more popular than anyone ever expected. Stricken with a sudden morality, Mary Wathen exited her bar contract in 1960 and moved back to Omaha. "I wanted no part of that, I didn't like the place and I never let Mr. Kaminsky forget it....I was the happiest gal in the world when it was sold. I could have danced in the street."

Kaminsky quickly recruited Wally Whetham to take over the license. They changed the name of the bar to the Black Nite. For Kaminsky's financial schemes to work, he needed a "useful idiot"—and he found one. Whetham made enough on the Black Nite to open a second bar, Captain's Cabin, later that year.

The Black Nite wasn't just a tavern that tolerated homosexuals; it was, from the start, a tavern that embraced and welcomed them. Whetham created a safe and generous space for his customers. All sexual and gender expressions were welcome—something extremely rare to find in 1960 Milwaukee—and customers were fiercely protective of their turf.

That fierceness made itself known on Saturday, August 5, 1961.

After losing a drinking bet at a Kane Place tavern, four twenty-year-old servicemen (Kenneth Kensche, John Cianciolo, Bruce Pulkkila and Edward Flynn) were sent to the Black Nite on a humiliating dare. When asked to show identification and sign a log, they panicked. Nobody was supposed to know they'd ever been inside a gay bar. They refused to cooperate and attacked the bouncer.

Josie Carter was one of two other people in the bar. Minutes earlier, she and her bouncer boyfriend were enjoying music and a cocktail. Now he was under attack. Josie instinctively grabbed a beer bottle and joined the fight.

"We didn't start anything, but we sure as hell finished it," said Josie Carter in 2011. "In that moment, I could fight off an army in a bathrobe. I let him have everything that was in that bottle. He went down."

The servicemen fled the bar, took their injured friend to the hospital and went back to the Kane Place tavern. They rounded up a dozen men and decided to go back downtown and "clean up the Black Nite."

"The owner said, we need to get you out of here, those guys are coming back with guns, and I said absolutely not," Josie would later recall. "I will not leave. We do not run from a fight. We do not run from anything."

As the Saturday night crowd rolled in, Josie shared the story with every single customer. The Black Nite had been their safe and accepting space in a cruel world. Now, the hate was here on their doorstep. Were they going to sit back and take that?

Earlier that night, the servicemen had found a nearly empty bar. When they returned, they found a packed bar of seventy-five patrons ready and willing to defend their turf by any means necessary. The battle didn't last long, but it was intense. In the end, over $2,000 in losses were reported, including the bar's entire bottled liquor inventory, an electric organ, a jukebox and all windows.

Josie remembered the Black Nite as one of the first bars to welcome "queens." *Wisconsin LGBTQ History Project.*

"She knew her very existence was criminal, her actions could have extreme social and legal consequences, and she may even be killed. But Josie Carter did not run from a fight," said Dr. Brice Smith of the Wisconsin Transgender Oral History Project.

"On the great game board of Wisconsin LGBTQ history, all the dominoes lead back to the Black Nite," said Don Schwamb, founder of the Wisconsin LGBTQ History Project. "Nothing was ever quite the same again after that night."

The Black Nite Brawl, as it became known, triggered immediate and significant cultural change in Milwaukee. News coverage of the Black Nite Brawl continued for more than a week and created a local "gay panic." Few local people knew an actual homosexual person in 1961, so the assumption was that they only existed in faraway big cities. People suddenly realized there were gay people here in Milwaukee, in large numbers, who would defend themselves if provoked. The stereotype of the passive, docile, weak homosexual was replaced by the widespread fear of an angry, violent, fearless homosexual.

In 1964, the *Milwaukee Journal* commented that "the homosexual has gotten bolder." The *Milwaukee Sentinel* was forced to agree: "Whether or not there are more of them than ever before, or if they're just become more visible…society at large needs to decide what it's going to do about the homosexual problem."

The panic accelerated efforts to build the long-awaited 794 freeway and erase these unwelcome homosexual haunts. The Black Nite Brawl haunted the property for months, affecting the bar's business and reputation, and Whetham was urged by the Common Council to change the business name and keep his liquor license. The bar operated as Bourbon Beat until being razed for St. Paul Avenue's extension in 1966. Between 1966 and 1967, Whetham lost both his bars, suffered a catastrophic bankruptcy and was implicated in the gruesome murder of his thirty-year-old "adopted son," James Spencer. He died alone in Upstate New York only ten years after the Black Nite.

The Black Nite was a call to arms for many emerging community leaders, including Eldon Murray and Alyn Hess, founders of Gay People's Union. It was the first time a gay bar was so openly identified in the newspaper. Like many men of their generation, they sought out news stories mentioning gay people and places throughout their childhoods, only to find negative indictments of gay people as "criminals," "perverts" or "sexual deviants." For the gay rights generation, the Black Nite offered a glimmer of hope and a spark of revolution.

This was more than a social revolution. The LGBTQ community was officially politically activated. By 1970, multiple LGBTQ groups had formed in Milwaukee: Gay Liberation Organization, a student-led organization supported by UWM professor Barbara Gibson; Gay Liberation Front, a sex-positive activism-driven group; and Radical Queens, an early trans liberation collective. GLO renamed itself Gay People's Union in February 1971 and reorganized as a community-based, non-student group in September 1971. Other gay groups formed by 1972, including Les Petit Bons Bons, the PTA (a gay dinner club) and the New Gay Underground (born from the smoldering ashes of the Gay Liberation Front).

While many of these groups did not survive more than a few years, Gay People's Union delivered many LGBTQ community "firsts" for Milwaukee, advocated for the nation's first Gay Rights Bill and founded BESTD Clinic as a critical population health resource. After its political victories were eclipsed by the AIDS crisis, GPU lost momentum and effectively disappeared by the mid-1980s. However, the organization was still technically incorporated as of its fiftieth anniversary in 2021.

Radical Queens were part of a national movement rejecting discrimination, oppression and stereotyping of transvestites, transsexuals and casual cross-dressers. Their semi-serious agenda supported radical politics (gay separatism, free sex changes, STAR, the Viet Cong, the Black

Panther Party and Cuba,) counterculture icons (Oscar Wilde, Angela Davis, Janis Joplin, Alice Cooper and Jane Fonda), local gay bars (The Rooster, The Buckskin) and "queerish" activities (baton twirling, roller skating, fur coats, ostrich feathers and dope).

"Radical Queens is a group of screaming sillies," read a 1971 manifesto. "We are a bunch of ferocious fairies. A heap of battling butterflies. A clump of conniving characters. A bundle of barbaric bitches. A panful of paranoid pornographic pansies. A fearsome few of flaming faggots. We're angry queens that are out to get you. And when we do, we're gonna set your hair aflame and scratch your eyes out, fuckers!"

Little is known about the organization, its leaders or its inspiration, outside of a pivotal meeting with Sylvia Rivera and Marsha P. Johnson of STAR at a Black Panthers convention in Philadelphia. This meeting was funded by the sale of stained-glass windows from Ogden Avenue homes scheduled for demolition for the Park East freeway. Radical Queens disbanded sometime before 1972, when they were replaced by New Gay Underground for another year.

"For more than fifty years, Carter was encouraged time and again to recount the night she fought off homophobic instigators and led her queer bar-mates in defending one of the few city spaces where they were free to be," said Dr. Brice Smith of the Wisconsin Transgender Oral History Project. "In her more senior years, this story took on the feel of folklore, and some came to question whether or not this could have ever possibly happened."

"Unlike the Stonewall and Compton's Cafeteria riots, the Black Nite Brawl did not pit queer and trans people of color against the police," Smith said. "Milwaukee police stood with their friend Josie on the right side of history, rounding up the queer community's attackers." Unfortunately, Judge Christ T. Seraphim would later dismiss the charges against the sailors.

Many of the first generation inspired by the Black Nite lost their lives to AIDS, leaving an ever-shrinking group of aging survivors with firsthand remembrances of the uprising. Carter died in 2014 without accepting any formal recognition for her pivotal role in changing Wisconsin LGBTQ history.

On the sixtieth anniversary of the Black Nite Brawl, the Wisconsin LGBTQ History Project officially commemorated its historic and cultural impact. Josie Carter and the Black Nite patrons were honored with official proclamations from Governor Tony Evers, Milwaukee County executive David Crowley, Milwaukee mayor Tom Barrett, the Milwaukee County

Board of Supervisors and the Milwaukee Common Council. It was the first time a queer trans woman of color received historical recognition in the state of Wisconsin. Efforts to install a historic sidewalk marker at the site are underway.

Before Stonewall ever happened, three dozen gay bars had opened in Milwaukee. One of these was Castaways (424 West McKinley Avenue), celebrated in national gay guides for "(same-sex) dancing permitted, almost encouraged" seven years before any Chicago bar allowed it. Others included Your Place (813 South First Street), the first gay bar owned by a gay couple; Nite Beat (multiple locations), a multigenerational women's bar where cultures really clashed between "old school butch" and "new wave feminism"; Godfrey's 1800 (1800 West Vliet Street), which ran the city's only all-Black drag shows throughout the 1960s; and This Is It (418 East Wells Street), open to this day as Wisconsin's longest-running gay bar.

The Black Nite inspired Milwaukee in another, most unexpected way. Queens—formerly a risk that most taverns wouldn't tolerate—were now the talk of the town. Drag shows, formerly seen as square, old-time entertainment, were back in style. Unlike earlier eras, fabulous female impersonators weren't sweeping into town from bigger cities. By 1969, the new generation of Milwaukee "queens" had restored long-lost gender and sexual liberties, created the first local drag celebrities and would soon welcome the return of the drag cabarets.

THE LURE OF THE BATON

By the end of the 1960s, "Moe" Monaco's Blue Dahlia was no longer attracting curious customers—or potential performers—from the Tristate Area. After the Chesterfield was raided in 1966, Chicago essentially banned drag for five full years. Some drag bars quietly continued, including the Nite Life (933 North State Street, 1969–1973) and the Isle of Capri (14511 Western Avenue, 1968–1974).

"The Nite Life was mostly hookers; entertainers were mostly strippers that went out with the trade, and gave the owners a cut of their profits," said Jim Flint.

Female impersonators weren't getting rich anywhere. But soon, a new type of nightclub would elevate drag to an aspirational career choice.

Leveraging what he'd learned at mob-owned female impersonator bars like the Chesterfield, Sam's, Annex and the Normandy Inn, Jim Flint and three partners opened Smitty's Show Lounge at 430 North Clark Street in 1969. This historic business survives to this day as the Baton Show Lounge (4713 North Broadway), despite financial challenges, a 2006 zoning code fiasco, Flint's retirement and the bar's transfer of ownership and move to Andersonville.

"Those first years were rough," Flint said. "At that time, the River North area was a nameless and seedy area. We had SROs and wino bars all over. People were afraid to come down here—seedy hotels, prostitution hotels, transient bars. Bars where the women would get up and strip for a bottle of wine. It wasn't a pleasant area to be in back in 1969."

When Smitty left the business, Flint renamed the business the Baton. It became a gateway from 1969 onward for aspirational drag stars from rural Wisconsin, urban Milwaukee and the entire Chicagoland area.

"He turned drag into dignity, into an art form for those not always headed for stardom," said Chicago attorney Ralla Klepak.

TOUGH TIMES IN A DEAD DOWNTOWN

Albert Tusa, the "king of Milwaukee nightlife," died on February 15, 1968. Downtown was starting to swirl the drain. "Nightclubs can no longer compete with the sets, color and absolute top entertainment provided by television," said Tony Fazio in 1970, when Fazio's on Fifth closed. "Then the riots hit Milwaukee and the local citizenry seems to have boycotted downtown."

Not everyone had abandoned downtown. Far more liberated than any generation before them, young gay, lesbian and gender nonconforming people began gathering at twenty-four-hour downtown diners like the heavily queer Loop Café (601 North Fifth Street), the twenty-four-hour Belmont Hotel Coffee Shop (751 North Fourth Street) and Marc's Big Boy (Fifth and Wisconsin) as early as 1963. Unfortunately, the large groups of gay youth were just seen as another symptom of a sick downtown.

"That's how we found out about gay places back then: meeting people and sharing stories," said Samantha Stevens. "A lot of gay people hung out on Wisconsin Avenue, so we'd walk up and down the street to find them. There are a lot of people still alive who got into the gay community at that Big Boy!"

"The Loop Café was lots and lots of gay people," said Chuckie Betz.

We were there because we couldn't get into bars, and dozens and dozens of gay kids would meet up there and at Marc's Big Boy. But the Loop was pretty loose, so you could fag out, and they'd allow it. There was an older crowd there, and they weren't happy with us youngsters. They were used to a world that was either butch or femme, and then along came us, younger, more out there, and less strict about these rules. So, the older gay crowd didn't like us, because we weren't the right kind of gay. And the hippies didn't like us because we were gay. You can't imagine how fast things were changing, it was such a time of transition.

In November 1977, the *Milwaukee Journal Insight* took a deep dive into the lives of four anonymous "transsexuals," stating that these individuals usually found their way into the lifestyle at "old homosexual haunts like the Loop Restaurant."

The Radical Queens, consisting of core members Eva Cream, Connie Worm and Angelo Peaches, were a common sight at downtown department stores, hotels, restaurants, movie theaters, civic events and even religious revivals.

"We were doing drag as confrontation, drag as terrorism, drag as genderfuckery," said Chuckie Betz aka Eva Cream.

Milwaukee was so sensible and so serious. We knew we had to shake that up. Our street drag was one dash man, one dash woman, some jewelry and a lot of make-up. We'd crash events when people least expected it. We crashed a Cudahy high school musical in huge fur hats, high heels, huge furry purses. The police were called, and we got kicked out, but it was worth it to be seen. We crashed a Job's Daughters event at the Marc Plaza Hotel. We jammed into the elevators and rode up and down. Some guy asked, "What are you, some kind of faggot?" and our natural response was "Why? Are you hard?" We weren't afraid of anything or anyone. We were so out there; we must have looked like aliens to normal people. I once appeared before a judge, and he sent me to a psychiatrist, stating "there must be a problem with me" based on my appearance. I was in full drag and my attorney—a woman—was in a man's suit.

Older drag queens were NOT okay with the confrontation drag. They thought it was making fun of them. I was once pushed into a pond by a group of three performers!

The nearby Royal Hotel had become so seedy that Milwaukee County considered acquiring the property to house maximum-security prisoners. The long-running Gay 90s bar was condemned and quickly demolished in

The Radical Queens challenged the queer status quo with "confrontation drag." *Wisconsin LGBTQ History Project.*

1968. After the abandonment of nearby train lines and depots, the Royal found itself in a purposeless corner of downtown. While the Balistrieri family sought to acquire the property for vice purposes, city boosters just wanted it gone.

For the umpteenth time, the Royal Hotel went bankrupt in 1968. Hopeful investors attempted an ill-advised rebranding of the Royal Hotel, including a new paint job, a modernized bar and a new steakhouse. Local gays mocked the hotel's attempt to become respectable (i.e., heterosexual). "The Buckskin Inn" debuted in 1969, failed miserably and was back in business as the Royal Hotel in 1971.

In 1971, Chuck Cicirello opened one of his first ventures, the Stud Club, in the Royal Hotel Bar. It was the first gay bar in Milwaukee to mix go-go boys and drag shows. The Stud Club folded after a year, and Chuck moved on to open the Neptune (1100 East Kane Place) in 1972 and the Factory (158 North Broadway) in 1973.

Michelle, a trans woman from St. Louis, opened a five-day-a-week drag cabaret at the Royal Hotel in 1972. She partnered with Winnie Storm, the reigning hostess of the era, to produce a blockbuster floor show. Many shows featured a dozen queens or more. Michelle's Club 546 included two salons, one with a twenty-four-hour coffee bar and one with late-night bar food until 5:00 a.m. Michelle's elderly "husband," Sam Mazur, held the licenses and properties on paper.

"I really enjoyed the vibe at Michelle's," said Samantha Stevens.

It was a really nice, up-to-date kind of place, with a restaurant across the lobby. We would all go to that restaurant and drink coffee for hours, gossiping about everything that was going on. I was dating Bill, a bartender who lived in the Royal Hotel penthouse. This was an actual mansion, built on the roof for the original owner, and after all those years it was still sitting up there. We would have to take people up in the elevator to prove it really existed. It was huge!

And then I won the Miss Michelle's 1973 pageant! It was funny, because I was up against older people, who had done drag long before me. Michelle and the older queens were glaring at me, like why did SHE win?

Here's what I think. My look was modern, natural, glamorous. I didn't look like a female impersonator. I just looked like a glamorous woman.

These older queens were so serious, so joyless. They looked like 1920s and 1930s Hollywood, with none of the mystique. Drag is about the performance AND the appearance. That's real talent. I knew that way back then.

Over her long career in
Milwaukee, Samantha Stevens
went from star to showrunner.
Sam Saglin.

*I didn't take the title, though, because you had to go back and do the
whole thing over the next year, and hand over your title and crown. At the
time, we didn't know there wouldn't be a next year for Michelle's. I went
back to Ohio. So, they gave first place to Mickey Chanel instead.*

*Mickey Chanel was one of the first Miss Gay Wisconsins, and one of
the most beautiful queens I'd ever seen, and she won everything she went out
for. Except, the one time I ran against her!*

Michelle's flourished until 1973, when the Royal Hotel was finally seized
by the city for redevelopment. Blue Cross Blue Shield demolished the
property in early 1974. As the story goes, Sam and Michelle were offered a
vacant glass-plate shop at 235 South Second Street, where they opened the
Oregon House in 1976, later the Phoenix (1979–1993). After Sam died in
the building in 1993, Michelle struggled onward alone with Déjà Vu (1993–
1994). However, she became increasingly sick and could no longer manage
the business alone. She returned to St. Louis, where she either died of AIDS

in hospice or threw herself into the Mississippi River, depending on curious and conflicting accounts. Even more curious, later occupants of 235 South Second Street reported spectral sightings of an "old man in a red hat," shot glasses sailing down the bar and glasses falling off shelves and shattering. Perhaps Sam and Michelle never really left Milwaukee after all.

By 1975, Fifth and Michigan had become an open red-light district. The *Milwaukee Journal* reported that "prostitutes walk up and down 5th street in scattered groups, sometimes totaling dozens." Police complained that the Lib Bookstore (formerly the Loop Café) had transvestite hookers on the take.

THE EMERGING GAY VILLAGE

Although Milwaukee thought it had scattered the gay community to the winds, displaced bars began collecting in the nearly vacant 100 and 200 blocks of South Second Street by 1969. Within just a few years, Castaways, Nite Beat, Knight Owl Restaurant, the Rooster, the Seaway and the New Riviera Show Lounge had opened or reopened in this area. Nearby, the River Queen (402 North Water Street) opened in 1971, and the Cove (157 South First Street) followed in 1972. Gay guides warned about the "rough neighborhood," but the promise of six welcoming businesses operating within one block attracted a young, urban generation.

"It was my first time at Castaways," said Maryann, a Wisconsin LGBTQ History Project contributor. "I was very shy, and my guy friends told me to just march up to the prettiest girl in the place and ask her to dance. I surveyed the room and picked a gorgeous brunette, who very kindly declined my offer. My friends were cracking up. I had picked the beautiful Jamie Gays, award-winning queen of the era."

Castaways closed in July 1972. As the story has it, Otto Schuller fell in love with reigning club kid Jamie Gays and gave him the club, which was renamed "New Jamie's" in December 1972. With Jamie Gays as host and Josie Carter spinning records, New Jamie's was briefly the drag place to be. However, Otto Schuller died of a heart attack at age forty-nine in November 1973. The Seaway restaurant and New Jamie's closed at the end of the year. On St. Patrick's Day 1974, the Ball Game opened at 196 South Second Street.

The New Riviera Show Lounge (183 South Second Street) opened on June 30, 1972, with the noble intention of bringing drag back to greatness. The Dolly Revue, presenting a cast of eleven local impersonators, was

The Riviera Show Lounge was the Hamburger Mary's of the 1970s. *Wisconsin LGBTQ History Project.*

produced by "Norma Jean" Baker and choreographed by Mel Powers. The show featured the reigning stars—Winnie Storm, Mel Powers, Jerry Powell, Andretta, Mother Chris—performing the top songs of the era. Fans remember Mother Chris performing a show-stopping "Hello Dolly." Shows were offered at 10:30 p.m. and midnight every Friday, Saturday and Sunday. Performers sought to take drag back out of the gay bar and back into the mainstream through "guilty pleasure" brunch and dinner shows. Their schedules were aggressive, their productions were intimidating and their budgets were unattainable. This was a serious dinner theater, where reservations were required.

"At that time, drag queens hung out at the Ball Game and the Riviera Show Lounge," said Samantha Stevens. "For a short while, that was it for the drag scene. The Riviera was an interesting one. They were always struggling to find the budget for these gigantic, ambitious shows. They advertised in the paper and tried to bring in a straight audience. That was brave in the early 1970s. Straight people just did not go to gay places!"

Following a license change, the Riviera Show Lounge was renamed Dionysus. In April 1974, the cast was preparing its most ambitious number ever—an Easter show with a twenty-one-member cast and a five-figure budget—when the showrunner fired a queen who wasn't keeping time. The fired queen demanded to be reinstated by Saturday night or she would set fire to the bar. "I'll burn this place to the ground before I let this show go on without me," so goes the story. Showrunners and cast members rolled their eyes and went on with rehearsals.

Early in the morning hours of April 22, 1974, a fire erupted in the dumpsters behind the bar. Little did the arsonist know that these dumpsters contained flammable chemicals from the nearby Courteen Seed factory. Rather than setting a mere fire, the arsonist set off a firestorm that consumed not only Dionysus but also the Flame (181 South Second Street), a garage at 179 South Second Street, a vacant building at 175 South Second Street and a portion of the Seaway Restaurant (173 South Second Street). Almost fifty years later, the arsonist remains unknown, and all that remains of Milwaukee's second great gay village is Just Art's Saloon at 181 South Second Street, which removed the entire second floor of the structure.

BIRTH OF THE PAGEANTS

The 1968 art film *The Queen* was influential in introducing Middle America to the concept of competitive drag. It introduced celebrity queens Flawless Sabrina, Pepper LaBeija and Dorian Corey. However, the film wasn't shown anywhere in Milwaukee until November 1971, when it debuted at the Billie Shears Film Society (911 East Ogden Avenue).

Milwaukee was ready for it. In 1970, Tiger Rose, Mama Rae, Ken W and John created MGM: Miss Gay Milwaukee to showcase the city's ever-growing drag community. Each of Milwaukee's ten gay bars would promote its own title competitions, host unique and exclusive performances and advance one winner to the citywide title pageant. The first three contests were at Castaways South (1971), the Neptune (1972) and the Factory (1973).

How were there possibly enough female impersonators in Milwaukee in 1970 to staff ten separate drag contests? Behold the cultural impact of the Black Nite and the earlier onset of gay liberation.

Samantha Stevens remembers the ruling queens of the era: Tiger Rose, Billie Shephard, Andretta, Duchess, Josie Carter, Jamie Gays, Mama Rae, Brandy Alexander, Ricki Vegas, Vicky Renee, Peaches Toy, the Powell Sisters, Stormy Weather, Mother Chris. "And probably two dozen more who only appeared once!"

"Tiger Rose was the ruling glamour queen," said Samantha. "Sometimes, she looked exactly like Kim Novak, and other times like Sheree North. I was fascinated with her. She held herself with such dignity, such grace. It was often difficult to believe she was not a woman."

"There were so many queens—it seemed like more and more every time you went out—and they would all talk about these pageants with such reverence," said Samantha. "The pageants were the biggest social event of the year. I was fascinated by the costumes and performances and so inspired by these stories. So, I started doing drag myself."

Believe it or not, the 1973 Miss Gay Milwaukee pageant welcomed not only the finalists but also a floor show that also employed twenty-seven backup performers. GPU News noted, "After an extremely late start, the lengthy show was replete with more production numbers than the Great White Way. The night just went on and on, only stopping abruptly a few moments before closing time to announce the winners." Sandi Alexandra was crowned the winner by exiting 1972 champion Billie Shepherd. Miss Joey presented a 25 Year Friendship Award to Josie Carter, who took first runner-up.

In 1973, the contest became Miss Gay Wisconsin and moved to the brand-new Factory nightclub.

The Factory (158 North Broadway) immediately elevated gay nightlife to a whole new level. Offering over 2,400 square feet of dance space, the Factory brought New York–level nightclubs to a tavern town, with a large light-up dancefloor, light shows, mirrored walls and a remarkable sound system. "If you want to make it, make it at The Factory" was the slogan, and they meant it: phones on tables circling the dancefloor allowed shameless flirtations with unsuspecting victims all night long. The Marquee Bar (later known as the Loading Dock) offered a 1,500-square-foot side stage where artists Tiger Rose and Mama Rae hosted drag shows, variety shows and full stage productions.

"It was the top gay bar in all of Milwaukee. There had never been anything like it. All the queens would come in drag on Friday and Saturday nights, not even to perform, just to see and be seen," said Sam. "They started doing these shows in the backroom—Tiger Rose, Mama Rae, Tina Capri—but I would just go with Miss Donny for drinks and people-watching."

"There might have been drag shows at other places in the early 1970s, but I only remember seeing them at the Factory," said Diane, a Wisconsin LGBTQ History Project contributor. "The Factory was so mixed: it wasn't uncommon to see women there, whether they were queens, femmes, fag hags, it didn't matter. All kinds of people were there, and everyone just fit into this big, wild, crazy family."

One fateful night, Diane graduated from being part of the audience to part of the cast. "Tiger Rose was doing a show, and from the stage, she pointed at me and asked if I was a girl or a boy!" Diane remembered. "Later, she said to my friend Pat and I, 'we've seen you and your friends dancing, and you're really quite good. Have you two ever thought about being in our shows?'"

The Factory hosted some of the earliest Miss Gay Milwaukee pageants. *Wisconsin LGBTQ History Project.*

"They were really doing shows just for fun. They'd decide, 'we're doing this show,' and we'd buy the album, pick our parts, rehearse our numbers, and go live a few days later! They really put their heart and soul into these little shows: the music, the moves, the set, the costumes."

Diane remembers her first Entertainers Club show in 1975, which featured Mel Powell, DeDe Darnell, Mother Chris, Tiger Rose, Mama Rae, Riki Vegas and Jerry Powers.

The Entertainers Club performed extravagant productions at the Crystal Palace (1925 West National Avenue), formerly the Knights of Pythias Castle Lodge, built by a German fraternal organization in 1921.

"These were some big hair, big costume numbers," said Diane. "Mama Rae and Tiger Rose would show up with five wigs and a rack of dresses each. I had a little suitcase on my lap. Things sure have changed since then."

"One of the reigning queens was Mother Chris," said Diane. "I actually lived in her house at Pleasant and Jackson Streets for a few months, which was very unusual, because Mother Chris did NOT like girls at all. She was old, crochety and cranky. I remember her sewing costumes and doing hair for local musician Dawn Koreen."

Some of Diane's other acquaintances from the Factory era included pageant winners Mickey Chanel and Vicky Renae, among the first trans women to have gender affirmation surgery in Milwaukee. She remembers visiting Riki Vegas at his coffee shop on Water Street. She also remembers Mama Rae's secret ingredient for the perfect bosom: bird seed!

By 1976, the Entertainers Club had grown to more than fifty members, and they took ownership for the production and promotion of the Miss Gay Wisconsin pageant. Pageant Productions took over in 1980 and renamed the contest Mr. and Ms. Gay Wisconsin. For ten years, the Entertainers Club called the Ball Game (196 South Second Street) their "home bar." The group disbanded in 1983.

Despite early gay pride events in 1973 and 1974, the pageant was the largest annual gay gathering in Milwaukee from 1975 to 1990. The event moved to the Centre Stage dinner theater (624 North Second Street) in 1975, where it would remain until October 27, 1979. The Centre Stage was the scene of traveling female impersonator shows throughout the 1970s, as well as innumerable gay-friendly performers, including Carol Channing, Martha Raye, Milton Berle, Paul Lynde, Liza Minnelli and Mary Tyler Moore. French Dressing, a Jewel Box–level touring drag show that made Milwaukee uncomfortable with its "AC/DC agenda," played here in July 1975.

The Centre Stage, located inside the Antlers Hotel, was demolished on December 21, 1979. For fifty-five years, the Antlers had been a SRO sanctuary for single gay men, but it had no place in a rapidly redeveloping downtown. The Pageant moved to the Crystal Ballroom of the Marc Plaza Hotel (now the Milwaukee Hilton) until 1990. Each year, it was larger, more sophisticated and more outrageous.

Vicky Renae and Mickey Chanel (aka Chanel Capri) were extremely popular performers in the early 1970s. *Wisconsin LGBTQ History Project.*

THE AD LIB REWRITES ALL THE RULES

Clever businessmen knew there was serious money to be made in the Sexual Revolution. On May 22, 1967, Le Bistro (821 North Third Street) joined a growing red-light district that already included the Brass Rail (744 North Third Street), the Downtowner Bar (340 West Wells Street), the Princess Theater (738 North Third Street) and many adult bookstores. What had been Milwaukee's Theater Row was quickly becoming a city of night. And Le Bistro, offering Sir Lady Java and the Third Sex Revue, was part of the darkening.

The nearby Ad Lib (323 West Wells Street) opened in June 1966 as a top-tier jazz club, dinner theater and steakhouse. It was ten years too late to survive in a rapidly racier downtown. Within its first year, the highly regarded nightclub welcomed Miles Davis, Thelonious Monk, Wes Montgomery, Dizzy Gillespie, Count Basie, Herbie Mann, Lionel Hampton, Dorothy Donegan, Henny Youngman, Rusty Warren, Art Van Damme, Gene Krupa and many, many more. Secretly owned by the Balistrieri crime family, the Ad Lib was making money hand over fist.

In August 1967, the Ad Lib shifted to an all-striptease format. "We're only doing this temporarily," promised manager Jimmy Jennaro. At the time, strict ordinances made it illegal for female entertainers to sit at any table, in any booth or elsewhere on the premises of a tavern with a male customer, or for performers to solicit drinks from anyone of the opposite sex. Female performers—including singers and musicians—were not allowed to accept drinks from the audience, although their male companions were encouraged to do so.

This didn't stop the B-Girls at the Ad Lib, who were as famous for drink hustling as they were for losing their tops. Hostesses hawked private meetings between dancers and patrons that were little more than wallet heists. Easy marks saw their twenty-dollar bills disappear as the giggling gals double-fisted shot after shot of overpriced "liquor" (aka seltzer water) and raced back to the dressing room.

The Ad Lib became known for remarkably racy floor shows. "Vice squads are cracking down on strip clubs," said the *Milwaukee Sentinel*. "The city allows dancers to strip down to their underwear, but at the Ad Lib, many dance in G-strings or less." Shortly thereafter, a dancer was arrested for appearing bottomless on stage, and another was arrested for "inappropriately" touching a police officer.

The Ad Lib was actively pushing its limits. Randy Taylor, formerly of the Jewel Box Revue, accepted a residency as the "Brazen Bombshell" of the Ad Lib in 1967. Her look was described as "half Jayne Mansfield, half Nancy Sinatra, and all-woman sex appeal." Teri Tyler of the Jewel Box Revue headlined an Ad Lib show in 1968 that was extended to eight weeks.

By the end of the year, six more striptease clubs opened within walking distance of the Ad Lib. With the bar business in the frying pan, the Ad Lib fearlessly jumped into the fire. Without a blink, management launched a surprising new lineup in early 1969. One night, the Ad Lib reassigned its regular girls to the Brass Rail and announced three new "Go-Go Girls" would replace them.

"Now appearing: The Third Sex!" yelled the emcee, "an all-star cast of female impersonators!"

Randy Taylor, the "brazen bombshell" of the Ad Lib, found herself at the center of a torrid murder trial. *Wisconsin LGBTQ History Project.*

"I was a stripper there for eight years," said Jamie Gays, who auditioned at the Ad Lib with crime boss Frank Balistrieri himself. "After I danced for him, he said 'you start tonight.'"

"During the Vietnam War, guys would throw their dog tags up on the stage. I'd charge them a dollar to get them back, but not until I rubbed them all over my tits and my pussy. If they knew that I was a guy, they would have killed me. No doubt about it."

"I worked with five entertainers, and they were all guys, except one girl who had the surgery. They were all guys except for one: Misty!"

Misty Dawn, a transgender performer billed as "The World's Most Beautiful Boy," quickly became the star of the floorshow. "Is She a 'He' or a 'She?'" screamed the ads. With a stage presence that was bigger than life, Misty brought big-city Chicago burlesque that audiences would never forget.

"She twists and wriggles to the tune of a scratchy record," reported the *Milwaukee Journal*. "Wearing only a G-string and a mesh bra, Misty squirms towards the stairway leading off stage. With a suggestive smile over her shoulder, she unfastens the G-string and wiggles it off. She flips it over her shoulder and makes a naked posterior exit up the stairs and out of sight."

Switching out the cast was smart business for the Ad Lib. The nightclub was busier than ever, with a sexually charged mix of clueless straights, clued-in gays, made men, vice cops and FBI detectives. The female impersonators were far cheaper talent than national jazz performers or burlesque dancers. Gay men were loyal customers, generous spenders and less likely to cause trouble. And the flexible gender identities of the performers provided a flexible defense as the Ad Lib's owners continued to push legal boundaries.

Best of all, the Ad Lib provided a rare and wonderful opportunity for Milwaukee "queens" (ranging from drag queens to transgender pioneers) to earn a commendable income in a safe and guarded space. Like the stars of the Jewel Box, the Ad Lib Girls were carefully protected moneymakers.

"A girl could make it big at the Ad Lib," said Jamie Gays. "She might even become a national act. The Ad Lib was the place where you could get discovered, where you could get booked in Chicago or New York. There was always this feeling that somebody was going to get world-famous."

Samantha Stevens started working at the Ad Lib nightclub (323 West Wells Street) in the early 1970s. It was the first job she ever worked in female expression.

"Mickey Chanel got me the job," said Samantha. "The show was only two dollars, so the house was always full. There were so many horny sailors! They didn't even know these were female impersonators. They looked

LITTLE MISTY

Trans pioneer Misty Dawn lived by her own rulebook and rewrote the rules of Milwaukee nightlife. *Wisconsin LGBTQ History Project.*

THAT good. They had those men in the palm of their hands. And here I was, right in the middle of all that, trying to figure myself out."

During "the most unusual show of the century," Misty Dawn exposed her breasts and buttocks on January 20, 1970, and was promptly arrested. Misty insisted that she was born a man and had been surgically transformed into a woman. Ad Lib management argued that since Misty was born a man, it was legal for "him" to dance topless and/or bottomless, sit with male patrons and solicit drinks.

As bizarre as it must have seemed in 1970, this was a genius defense. The City of Milwaukee had long maintained that female impersonators were subject to the same regulations as female entertainers. Now, city attorneys struggled to compose charges, since they were technically unable to determine if Misty had displayed male or female anatomy. "Attorneys couldn't decide whether to refer to Misty in the complaint as 'He,' 'She,' or 'It,'" awkwardly reported the *Milwaukee Journal*. "They finally settled on 'You.'"

Local reporters pondered: would Misty's anatomy be subpoenaed by the court? The Ad Lib brilliantly banked on the scandal, inviting patrons to "Come See the Talk of the Town—Every Last Inch of Her!"

In the end, Misty got off with a fifty-dollar fine, but the publicity had rightly earned her (and the Ad Lib) a considerable amount of money. And she wasn't the only Ad Lib Girl making headlines.

When Randy Taylor launched a torrid Hotel Wisconsin affair with wealthy industrialist August Berganthal, she found herself the star witness in the most sensational local murder trial of the 1960s.

She refused a subpoena to testify about Berganthal's sexual identity. When a Milwaukee police officer tried to apprehend her at the Hotel Wisconsin, she punched him in the face and escaped in a closing elevator. She quickly vanished from Milwaukee, claiming that the stress of the trial had caused her great physical anxiety. Subjected to a body attachment warrant, the female illusionist refused to testify without a $25,000 retainer.

Attorneys were attempting to use a homosexual relationship as evidence of Berganthal's total insanity. Local reporters were as impressed by fashions as they were by the revelation that Berganthal paid for her breast enhancement surgeries.

Randy Taylor vanished after the trial. She was last memorialized in a 1981 issue of *Les Girls* celebrating the "Stars of Yesteryear." Although several researchers have tried to locate Randy or confirm her final resting place, none has ever been successful.

It all became a cautionary tale about what could happen to wayward husbands who wandered into the Ad Lib, despite having nothing to do with the crime at hand.

TEMPLE STAR, "THE WORLD'S greatest female impersonator," aka Dana Andrews, was arrested on March 27, 1969, after stabbing his roommate several times. "Police said both men were charged with lewd and lascivious behavior because they lived together as Mr. and Mrs. Richard Andrews."

Everyone, from the Milwaukee Police Department to the attorney general, publicly vowed to shut down the Ad Lib. You wouldn't know it from the number of vice cops who regularly patronized the bar, drinking for free all night long. When questioned, they would only give the name of their superior officer, who in turn would give out his.

"Apparently [the nightclub] feels it can operate with impunity," said District Attorney E. Michael McCann. "Let us be clear. The Ad Lib features female impersonators. It hardly adds anything to our community."

The Third Sex shows, which started as a clever legal loophole, had become a lightning rod liability. "All-Girl" shows came back to the Ad Lib marquee. Although few of the impersonators left the lineup, the gender policing stopped. Bartenders lamented that "excess numbers of homosexual customers" had taken their money elsewhere.

The liquor license quietly expired on June 30, 1975. The Balistrieris found a useful idiot to take out a new license, and the Ad Lib crawled along until the end of the year. In its final weeks, the Ad Lib returned to female impersonators and showcased Miss Gay Milwaukee Mickey Chanel. The gilded gold and scarlet cabaret was shuttered for several years, until La Scala restaurant opened in November 1979 for a four-year run. It was the last hurrah for Balistrieri nightlife in Milwaukee.

THE DISCO YEARS

Disco and drag were neck-and-neck for nightlife popularity. In July 1976, the Circus Disco opened at 219 South Second Street and proclaimed itself "Milwaukee's first real disco" and its first real laser-light show in 1978. Three short-lived gay bars had earlier operated here, including Gallery Lounge (1974), Mister Z's (1975) and Gary's: A Bizarre Place to Boogie (1976). With drag hosts enchanting crowds under the cut-glass leaping lion, the Circus was the first real challenger to the Factory as the disco. Soon, the city was home to over thirty discos, including the nearby Park Avenue (500 North Water Street), Red Baron (625 East St. Paul Avenue) and Teddy's (1434 North Farwell Avenue), as well as bi-curious swinger havens like He & She (3555 South Twenty-Seventh Street) and the Interns (555 North Seventh Street).

Circus was elegant, decadent, colorful and vibrant—exactly what Milwaukee needed at the time—and managed to feel swank and sleazy in a good way. "Lively nightly crowd jams newly-refurbished den. Young. Disco your body up; lounge down; drinks in the middle," reported the 1977 Milwaukee Gay Guide. By October 1978, founders George and James had exited the business, and new owners "Mike" and "Rick" relaunched the disco as Club Circus, a membership card club. This didn't seem to work, and soon the bar was renamed Circus Circus and finally just Circus. Despite colorful events, the new concept lasted only about a year. Sadly, Circus disappeared from nightlife listings in late 1979.

The M&M Club (124 North Water Street) opened on July 4, 1976, as the final corner of the Third Ward "Fruit Loop." It began hosting live entertainment almost immediately.

"Ricki Vegas, an established drag queen, took Rona, Dee, Totie, and me under her wing and helped us put on the first show at the M&M," said Phillip (aka Patsy Parks). He continued,

> *Dee Dee and I played chorus boys as well as girls. Lannie Stoddard (Bob's partner at the time) and another young man that I can't recall his name played chorus boys in several numbers. We were just a bunch of talented kids looking for a creative outlet. I think we all had a little theater in our background and—for me at least—that was the draw to drag for me. I saw it as another facet of theater. And of course, you can see this manifest in the full musicals that Rona and I put on at the M., i.e.,* Chicago *&* Cabaret—*then later* Dames at Sea *with Doris Delago.*

Left: Rona, Miss Gay Wisconsin 1980, and her successor Patsy Parks. *Phil Parks*.

Below: Mr. and Miss Gay Wisconsin Pageant at the Marc Plaza Hotel. Winners (*center*) Lamarr and Patsy Parks. Ginger Spice was first runner up. *Phil Parks*.

The camaraderie was always my favorite part. Yes, there was a whole lot of "bitch" going on, but the truth is that the drag queens I knew were some of the kindest, most generous people that I've ever known. I loved being a part of that facet of our community. How did M&M Club and their shows become such a major part of LGBT life in the late '70s and early '80s? Timing! Rona and I both worked at the M&M and it was taking off. Bob Schmidt was extremely supportive and accommodating—at times rearranging food service to set up the stage and allowing Rona and I flexibility with our schedules to do the shows.

The restaurant did not have anything to do with it. In fact, we did many, many summer shows on the back patio just outside the restaurant. I do think there was a saturation point of drag in Milwaukee. At a point you could go to a drag show every night of the week in Milwaukee. Also, I pretty much retired when I passed on my crown in '81–'82. Rona still performed for years afterwards. I really don't think I was looking for a creative outlet any longer. There were other areas to channel that energy.

It took off! Then, I won Miss Wisconsin in '80–'81 and passed the crown to Rona in '81–'82. Because of the title we were not just doing shows at the M&M but at all bars (including the Wreck Room) around Milwaukee and all the way up to Green Bay and back down to Chicago and Rockford, Illinois. We gained a reputation, and people wanted to be at the M&M for the booze, food and entertainment. Right place—right people—right time.

I believe that the stars aligned at this special time in Milwaukee gay history. I know that everybody must feel this way about their lives—but that's OK. This was true for me. I met some incredible people and forged great friendships and have remained in touch with most of them throughout my life.

Drag also broke into the women's bars, including the Beer Garden (3743 West Vliet Street) and the Lost & Found (618 North Twenty-Seventh Street), which also offered high-quality gender-bending stage shows throughout the late 1970s and early 1980s. Shadows (814 South Second Street), one of Milwaukee's most fabulous gay dining experiences, also offered live drag entertainment on a regular basis.

5

THE GOLDEN AGE (1981–1990)

This is the '80s, darling. You're going to see a lot of things you've never seen before.

On July 12, 1979, Disco Demolition Night at Chicago's Comiskey Park unleashed a riot of racist and homophobic rage, as over fifty thousand rock fans stormed the stadium screaming, "Death to disco!" The event confirmed what Milwaukee nightlife already knew: discos were no longer a euphoric paradise that brought people of all races, genders and sexual orientations together. Disco—the music, the fashions, the lifestyle—had become increasingly uncool, even embarrassing.

Approaching its tenth anniversary, the Factory fell out of favor after a spree of high-profile police harassment. Despite short-lived relocations to 135 East Juneau (1982–1984) and 511 North Broadway (1986–1987), the Factory ultimately relinquished its title as the king of nightlife.

So, what would be the next big cultural phenomenon? Look no further than MTV.

THE RISE OF CLUB 219

Trash, a mysterious, sexually charged venture, advertised events in the old Circus space from August 1980 to January 1981, some featuring visiting performers from Eddie Dugan's Bistro in Chicago. Early ads mention "Trash: A High Energy Experience," while later ads invite customers to

Left: Performer on the bar at Club 219, the drag scene was changing. *Diana Mixalakopoulou.*

Right: Ginger Spice channeling Boy George on the famous stage at Club 219. *Diana Mixalakopoulou.*

"Trash It Up at Club 219." Was it a leather bar? A punk club? Something entirely different? It didn't last long enough to find out. On February 12, 1981, ads celebrated the grand opening of Club 219. This infamous dance and drag emporium would remain open for twenty-four years before closing in October 2005.

"We finally opened Club 219 in spring 1981," said Del. "This was after one failed attempt by Tony [Canfora] and Robert Uyvari to open under a sublease agreement in 1980. Trash was only open for three months."

"Drag shows were introduced as a way for us to tap into the Sunday bar-goers," he said. "It wasn't long after Park Avenue, a straight nightclub, began opening as 'Gay Night' on Sunday nights. Our decision angered the bars known as 'drag bars'—The Ball Game and M&M Club."

"Tony went down to the Baton Show Lounge in Chicago," said Del, "and being the schmoozer he was, he was able to employ queens from the Baton to highlight on a regular basis. He took trips to Acapulco to see the 'female impersonator' shows down there. He came back totally inspired to bring that high quality to the shows at Club 219. In addition, he incorporated the talents of artist Robert Uyvari to decorate and renovate the Club. Bobby was also the artistic director for some of the shows."

Scott LaFlex and Erica Stevens bring the heat to Club 219. *Diana Mixalakopoulou.*

"It was our intent to literally elevate the art of drag to new heights in Milwaukee, both in quality of production and in actual height. The stage was located over the middle of the club, with a twenty-foot ceiling, and the stage was four feet off the floor on the dance side and ten feet off the floor on the bar side."

"Tony and I also made sure the performers were lifted to higher standards," said Del. "We made sure the performers knew the words to all of their songs. We would not tolerate the old mouthing of 'peas and carrots' to fake the lip-synching. As the show progressed, we hired Ginger Spice as the show's director, and after Ginger died, that job went to B.J. Daniels."

> *At the beginning of the shows, Tony would also make sure the performers' costumes were of the highest quality. He even offered to pay for many a performer's gown!*
>
> *We were the first venue in Milwaukee to pay the queens. Previously, female impersonators had been used as a tool for benefits and events. In those instances, they would either be paid a percentage of the take or be expected to perform pro bono. Being paid a salary was encouragement to upgrade their wardrobe and set the standard for other bars. Eventually, they also paid for local talent.*

Opposite: Tina Capri in a colorful stage costume. *B.J. Daniels.*

Above, left: Shante (Alexandra Billings) of the Baton Show Lounge emotes at Club 219. *Lily White.*

Above, right: Bombshell Candi Stratton captured backstage. *Diana Mixalakopoulou.*

> *Throughout the renovations of the club, the stage became even larger, with enhanced lighting and a spotlight to improve not only the drag shows, but national performers including Gloria Gaynor, Taylor Dayne, the Village People, the Weather Girls and Divine.*

In April 1982, Karl Kopp celebrated the first anniversary of Elsa's (833 North Jefferson Street) with a special midnight show with girls from Club 219 and the Baton Show Lounge. "People just come here to be seen. I know I do!" said radio personality Bobby Rivers. "Elsa's is the Ma Maison of the Midwest. It's wonderful not to see people drinking out of beer cans."

"By the early 1980s, society had a changing perspective of the LGBTQ community," said Del.

> *There was a definite gay movement. Drag was something the community could call its own—uniquely. Drag was a way for the community to*

transcend the world around them, for a short while, and to escape to another world. Drag was also used as a tool to increase financial support for LGBTQ causes. During this same timeframe, the leather community began to emerge. In response, the drag community became more sophisticated and elegant.

My favorite performances were "Don't Tell Mama" from Cabaret *with the 219 Girls; "Here Comes the Rain Again," with the Uyvari rain feature; and "Don't Cry for Me Argentina," which Miss B.J. Daniels sang from the parapet of the stage. Anything with Ginger Spice—or Shante from the Baton, who sang live!*

The lure of the great stage at the Club 219 brought many performers from the Chicagoland area, including Alexandra Billings, Mimi Marks and Candi Stratton, who went on to become enormously famous. Each represented Wisconsin as queen following pageant victories in Milwaukee.

"I got my start in Milwaukee," said Candi Stratton.

I remember seeing Ginger, Abbey Rhodes, Gloria P. Hole and B.J. Daniels at Papagaio's. I introduced myself to Ginger. I felt she was the most approachable—I mean, she fell down the stairs during her number! After the show, she asked me to audition for the revue at Club 219.

After making that connection, a whole group of us auditioned for La Cage in Chicago, including Shante (Alexandra Billings), Patti Kakes, Gloria P. Hole, Ginger Spice and myself. Eventually, Patti, Shante and I became regular cast members at Club 219. I also became the first Miss Wisconsin Continental, the second Miss La Cage and Miss Club 219 1989. Soon afterwards, I took a break from performing to complete my transition. I came back in 2003 doing my Cher act in places all around the world, including Australia.

Richard "Ginger Spice" Wyatt (1960–1991) grew up in northern Illinois, where he worked at his family's businesses. He moved to Milwaukee in 1978. While working as a waiter at the Factory, Ginger was "discovered" by Tiger Rose to perform in his drag show. Tiger was Ginger's "drag mother" and taught him the ways of female illusion. Ginger returned to Illinois and worked in the family business by day while building out a massive drag following by night. Ginger became friends with Jim Flint of the Baton Show Lounge, who nominated Ginger to run the Miss Continental Wisconsin pageant. Over the years, Ginger would claim the titles of Miss Gay Wisconsin and Miss Chicago Continental. She returned to Milwaukee at exactly the right moment.

With a new cabaret in town, there was a tremendous need for fresh talent. And Samantha Stevens knew exactly where to find it.

"Ginger Spice was living about a block away from me on Fourteenth and Wells with another queen," said Sam. "We were all neighbors, so we got to be good friends, and eventually got to talking business. I said, hey, why don't we start something together? And that's how the Who's No Lady Revue got started."

Ginger Spice portrait. *Diana Mixalakopoulou.*

"They were just opening up Club 219 (219 South Second Street), and they asked me to become show director," said Sam. "And the Who's No Lady Revue was a powerhouse cast. We always had a cast of four to five girls, and we traveled all over doing shows. I booked the shows, I collected the money, I picked out the overtures, the whole business operation."

Who's No Lady was a superstar drag factory that launched some of the biggest names of the 1980s: Ginger Spice, Abby Rhodes, Coco Lopez, Josie Blake, Gloria P. Hole and Miss B.J. Daniels. Some of Sam's earliest favorite shows happened at Zak's, on Humboldt Avenue, and Niko's, the predecessor to La Cage.

"There had been drag shows before," said Sam, "but nothing like the shows we were putting together. These were true theatrical productions, top to bottom, start to finish, with high-quality standards. You didn't just go out there in a wig and a dress and lip sync. Oh no, no, no. You presented the full illusion until you became the illusion."

Samantha remembers traveling to Madison to recruit Miss B.J. Daniels, who was performing at Going My Way (111 West Main Street).

"She was just stunning," said Sam. "I was mesmerized by this beautiful blonde bombshell. I thought, hey, maybe she'll come with us to Milwaukee. And she did!"

MISS B.J. DANIELS

"I was Miss Gay Madison in 1980," said B.J. Daniels. "They saw my photo in one of the bar magazines and came out to see me. Back then, I was just 'B.J. from Madison,' I didn't even have a real name yet."

Everyone in the Revue had a role, and Sam told me that my role was going to be glamour queen. Tony and Dell had just opened Club 219, and they hadn't even remodeled yet—the interior was very different than what people remember today. I was traveling back and forth from Madison for the shows, but after a terrifying car accident, I was like no. I'm not doing this anymore.

Ginger said, "You're going to move in with Samantha," and so I did. I stayed on a studio bed in Sam's parlor, which had pocket doors I could close at night. We lived in this fabulous, three-story Victorian rooming house at 939 North Fifteenth Street that was filled with eccentric characters.

Sam introduced me to everyone in the world. I met a lot of older, more established people in the business because of him. I felt so embraced by this enormous community of talented performers and elders. I remember visits with Mel and Jerry at their Mineral Street home. They'd show us trunk loads of costumes in their attic from their glory days.

"Sam pioneered the idea of the high-glamour show," said B.J.

She would always remind us, you're not a drag queen, you are a female impersonator. Drag queens are obvious men. Drag queens are not artists, they just get dressed up and go out.

She put together a real variety show of people—and she made sure every single person looked stunning in every single number. Gloria P. Hole was a comedian, but she looked amazing doing comedy. Coco Lopez would do Carmen Miranda numbers, but she was always dressed to the nines. There was nothing tacky or cheap about the shows. That was Sam's claim to fame: she started a new trend for a new era, with a new cast of fresh faces, steeped in feminine glamour and illusion. She raised expectations and elevated the art of drag to new levels. People were so taken in by our performances, they would actually be surprised that we weren't women.

Sam got me a job at J.J. Garlic's. We were inseparable for an entire summer. I knew when it was time for me to leave the nest, so I moved to Brady Street after two to three months, and Coco Lopez got me a job at the Finlandia Spa.

Truth be told, I would not be here in Milwaukee today without my connection to Sam.

After three years at Club 219, the Who's No Lady Revue was raking in customers, but the bar owners questioned whether the partnership was worthwhile.

Above: B.J. does her makeup backstage. *Diana Mixalakopoulou.*

Left: B.J. Daniels, punk rock style, on a fire escape. *Francis Ford.*

Samantha and B.J. reunited in 2018. *Mike Hiller.*

La Cage cast, including Liz, Vanessa Alexander, Holly Brown and Mary Richards. *Mary Richards.*

"Some people complained, 'why do we need to pay Samantha when she doesn't host, and she doesn't perform? What is she actually doing?'" said B.J. "She was more than just our agent, more than a den mother. She was bringing the vision to life. That's what she was doing."

"People were always trying to undercut the girls," said Sam. "I always found myself in arguments with venue owners who didn't want to pay after a gig. Things got bad at Club 219, because the owners didn't like me. I was too outspoken—they wanted me to do as I was told. But that's just not me. One day, I told Ginger, here you go, take the reins. And I walked away. Ginger stayed there until she died. She produced beautiful, enchanting, heart-stopping shows with B.J. and the Club 219 Girls. I would still go to the shows and visit her upstairs afterwards. But I was done."

LA CAGE AUX FOLLES

La Cage Aux Folles (801 South Second Street) opened in Milwaukee on March 6, 1984. There was no connection to Chicago's ultra-popular La Cage (50 East Oak Street), which ran from 1980 to 1983 and launched Divine's nightclub act. The Who's No Lady Revue began performing at La Cage Aux Folles almost immediately. Samantha served as the bar's first show director for seven years.

"By the mid-1980s, the drag scene was fueled by the need to raise money for the AIDS crisis," said owner George Prentice. "We had some remarkable queens, including Holly Brown, Abby Rhodes, Erica Stevens, Kellie Lauren, Sage Larue, Josie Blake, Patty Cakes, Gloria P. Hole, so many more," said Corey Grubb.

On October 18, 1984, La Cage was accused of "skirting the law" by municipal court judge Christopher Foley. The district attorney originally charged operator Nicholas Stathas $500 but reduced the fee to $100 plus court costs. "Four men dressed as famous female entertainers were performing to taped music on June 6 and June 13, despite prior warnings," said the complaint. The court required La Cage to display a tavern amusement license, along with its tavern dance hall license. As of October 11, no tavern amusement license had been filed. Stathas argued that the entertainers were amateurs, that the performance was only a rehearsal and that the Who's No Lady Revue had been performing at Niko's for three years. The prosecution noted there was a "showtime" light illuminated outside.

Judge Foley wrote a five-page opinion after the three-hour hearing, in which he reflected that drag shows were an old Milwaukee tradition that La Cage was now carrying forward. "[Drag is] in the tradition of Milwaukee, it's part of the ethnic quality of this city. Many, many years ago, it was part of the Gemuetlichkeit, and people from the tavern audience were called up to sing."

It was the first and last time a La Cage drag show would be raided. Nearly thirty years later, the club is still running weekly shows.

ERICA STEVENS

In 1982, I was only eighteen years old. My first time out in drag was at Papagaio's (515 North Broadway), where B.J. and Abbey were doing weekend shows. Gloria P. Hole was a no-show. My group of friends—six of us BTW—actually discussed what we would do if they asked us to come onstage. I said I would do it. And then, she picked me out of the audience and asked me to come onstage. I was terrified! I agreed—and the rest is history. I was a 219 Girl within a couple of weeks.

KAREN VALENTINE

Quite honestly, I never thought of myself as a "drag queen." I still can't do face! I'm not quite sure what I do, once I'm out there on the boards, but it's been a love affair with the stage, the audience, the performers. Drag is about finding a place: a home. It's a place of acceptance, love and welcoming. It's a sorority of like-minded individuals, who have a shared love of performing this unique art form.

It's as if we are all aiming towards the same destination, yet we all have our own road. Yes, we've blazed our own trail—that has earned us friends, fans, even a family of sorts; and of course. We've also earned ourselves foes, who don't get our message, meaning or what we're all about...and that's fine. Not everyone will "get" you.

Since February 1986, my career has continued to grow and develop, as do I, I hope, as a person and as a performer. Yet I still want to maintain who I am, who I was, being genuine and being here and dedicated since the mid-1980s.

I still get giddy when invited to be in a show or to perform somewhere outside the box. I'm online ordained, so I've done weddings, birthdays,

Left: Erica Stevens, close up, backstage. *Diana Mixalakopoulou.*

Below: Karen Valentine, Milwaukee's favorite live drag cabaret performer. *Karen Valentine.*

retirement parties, destination celebrations, bachelor/bachelorette parties and a myriad of fundraisers. If memory serves me, that's what really launched Karen Valentine! The Gay Chorus, HIT, SSBL, CCF and countless HIV/AIDS fundraisers. Every entertainer from 1985 forward donated their time and talents. We were the pioneers raising money and awareness before it was in vogue.

All those memories flood back to me, looking at photos, costumes, sets, programs, after all these years, it's a "Collage of Images." They warm my heart, make me smile, remind me how I met friends—whom I'm still doing shows with today!

I'm at a time in my life, that the French refer to as "A Certain Age." I know we all have an expiration date stamped on us…but as long as I'm continued to be asked and invited to play, I'm going to continue to give it my all!

HOLLY BROWN (1945–1991)

Soon, La Cage and Club 219 were deadlocked in competition to produce the fiercest drag shows Milwaukee had ever seen. A Golden Age of Drag was in full effect. Competition raged so hard that employees and customers had to choose their loyalties to one venue over another. Performers were so highly regarded that they became Milwaukee royalty. Under the tight quality controls of Samantha Stevens, La Cage's shows were elevated to Broadway-level productions that attracted crossover crowds several nights a week.

La Cage's popularity continued to soar with the arrival of Holly Brown & Company shows in 1988, even as her close friend and former roommate Ginger Spice was taking Club 219 to new heights.

Holly Brown (aka Holly Brown Tongue) was a popular singer, comedienne, dancer and cabaret operator in 1980s Milwaukee. Her sizzling drag performances, individually and as part of Holly & Company, became a local sensation that drew large and loyal crowds, gay and straight alike. Today, the Holly Brown shows are remembered for their larger-than-life production quality and large ensemble casts, above and beyond almost anything Milwaukee had ever seen before in a drag show.

Holly was born in Dubbo, a small town in the Australian outback. She started her stage career at age fifteen and was known for her flair for costume design. She moved to Sydney to begin modeling, acting and working as a female impersonator. With the full support of her family, Holly Brown made

Left: Holly Brown onstage at Club 219. *Diana Mixalakopoulou.*

Right: Holly Brown, fantasy showgirl and lover of old school glamour. *Francis Ford.*

a name for herself throughout Australia. Soon, Holly began appearing in Europe and around the United States: Provincetown, Miami, New York, Chicago, San Francisco, Denver, Los Angeles and Milwaukee.

During an American tour, she met Ginger Spice (aka Richard Wyatt) in Chicago. They were briefly roommates in Libertyville, Illinois, before Holly moved to Milwaukee in May 1986.

Holly joined the 219 Girls, where Ginger was an original cast member, and remained there for about eighteen months. In January 1988, she moved to La Cage with Claim to Fame talent shows on Wednesdays and Holly & Company variety shows on Sundays, following an afternoon tea dance and evening buffet that made La Cage an all-day venue.

Soon, the Holly Brown shows expanded to Saturdays and filled seats three nights a week. The increasingly elaborate shows featured male, female and drag performers delivering a full range of entertainment: dance, comedy, theatrical renditions, solo vocal numbers and more.

"By the late 1980s, our crossover crowd was maybe 30 to 40 percent straight on Saturday nights," said George Prentice. "They'd come for the show, stay to dance and have the night of their lives."

Holly embraced her fine-arts roots in Milwaukee. She had operated Holly Art, a commercial art business in Australia. In November 1987, she hosted an art exhibition at the Leo Feldman Galleries. Her artwork often graced the cover of *InStep* magazine and other publications. She also designed the mural that decorated the now-closed Mother's Kitchen. She appeared in filmmaker Cathy Cook's project, *Bust Up*. She had a love of classic films that inspired many of her performances and productions.

After five years in Milwaukee, Holly decided it was time to go home. She bid an emotional farewell to Milwaukee in April 1990 with a gala performance at La Cage. In several moving performances, Brown thanked the people she had known, "the ones who made all this possible." And then, she was gone.

Holly planned to reunite with a group of Milwaukeeans in Europe in spring 1992 and then return to Wisconsin together afterward. However, Holly became seriously ill in fall 1991 with pneumocystis carinii pneumonia (PCP). She was discharged from Gold Coast Hospital in Miami, Queensland, in late September, only to reenter the hospital a few weeks later. She died there on November 16, 1991.

"She made people happy, even though her life was sometimes a little rough," said *InStep* magazine. "Her accent, her smile, her love and her bawdiness will be remembered and cherished by many." Sadly, Ginger Spice passed away only ten days later on November 26, 1991, at age thirty-one.

"It's always sad when our friends succumb to AIDS, but it hurts even more when they were vivacious entertainers, who brought smiles to our faces every time they performed," said Ron Geiman, *InStep* publisher. "We'd like to imagine Holly and Ginger are throwing a Reunion Special in heaven."

Group number at Club 219 with Ginger Spice, Tina Capri, Mama Rae, Holly Brown, B.J. Daniels and Tiger Rose. *B.J. Daniels.*

Milwaukee was losing so many stars, so fast, that the nights were becoming quite dark.

On December 18, 1985, Tiger Rose hosted her last show, a Christmas cabaret at the Danceteria (618 North Twenty-Seventh Street) that also featured Mama Rae, Bouji, Kelly Michaels and Tina Mitchell. No photos or reviews exist of this grand finale. Tiger Rose (Edward Shicker Jr.) died in 1989 at age fifty. His obituary credited Tiger Rose for driving wider acceptance of drag in Milwaukee:

> *Milwaukee saw female impersonation in a much more positive light, due to Eddie elevating "Halloween" events to events at the Performing Arts Center, Marc Plaza and Centre Stage Theater. He stressed the realistic rather than the false drag queen approach. He was a pioneer in live performances where queens sang with their real voices. He built the first stage at the Factory, complete with red velvet curtains, swag drapes and spotlights. He was famous for hosting three hour shows—and always starting and running late. He helped many, many people learn how to be proud about being gay.*

Tina Capri and Mama Rae left Milwaukee for Cleveland after Tiger's death. Both passed away in the late 1990s without any local commemoration.

LILY WHITE

Lily White, Duwanna Moore, Lady Miranda and Kylie West relax between shows at Wizards Pub. *Lily White.*

I started doing drag in the mid-'80s. One of the first times was obviously Halloween at La Cage! The first night I looked like Sally Fields. The next night, my boyfriend Ricky Becker and I had Goldie Adams paint our mugs. We looked fabulous! I was always a theater kid growing up, so I was not new to the stage.

With help from friends and mentors, Miss Lily White came to life. Without sisters like Baby Jane Hudson, Lady Miranda, Kyllie West, Mary Richards, B.J. Daniels and so many more, I don't know where I'd be today.

MARY RICHARDS

I started drag in 1988 in Milwaukee and retired from Minneapolis's the Gay 90s in 2000. Learning was really by watching drag shows. Also, MTV was so popular at the time. That was such a great way to learn and visualize.

I remember my La Cage sisters: Holly Brown, Goldie Adams and Vanessa Alexander. I remember my 219 sisters: B.J. Daniels and Ginger Spice. At 219, we were so lucky because girls from the Baton would come and work with us. I was always so in awe of them.

Without a doubt, Bjork's "Big Time Sensuality" was my favorite performance that I did. I could completely let loose and embody the character. In Milwaukee, the drag community was one big family. Even if you worked at another bar, we were all friends, always laughing and cheering each other on.

SHANNON DUPREE

Shannon Dupree broke into drag in March 1988. "My first time was a dare at Club 219," said Shannon. "Since then, I've worked at La Cage, Just Us, Hamburger Mary's This Is It, C'est La Vie, Harbor Room, Mona's, Tina's, Conversations, Purr and Rene's Cozy Corner."

Shannon considers her role models to be Tasha Long, Tommie Ross, Monica Monroe, Dominique Mahon and Ginger Spice.

EXIT, STAGE LEFT

After a decade of star-making and show-running, Sam stepped out of the business in 1991. "There were so many cliques," said Sam, "and I think the cliques kind of killed drag for a while. That's why I quit it all. I got sick of going to bars and having to deal with the drama. And truth be told, so many of my friends were dying. Ginger. Josie. Holly. So many more. One night I just said, 'My work here is done.' It's time to be in the audience now." The golden age was over.

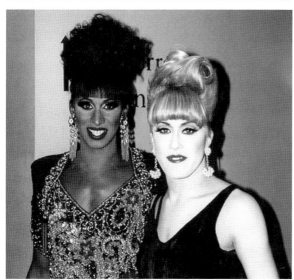

Top: Shannon Dupree performs with back-up dancers at PrideFest. *Howard Leu.*

Middle: Shawna Love and Shannon Dupree do a disco duet at PrideFest. *Howard Leu.*

Bottom: Duwanna Moore and Mary Richards: the high hair with bangs was a trend of the times! *Mary Richards.*

6

DRAG AND THE DISAPPEARING GAY BAR (1991–2008)

It wasn't easy, no one, two, three. Took a long time to learn to feel free.

Club 219 remained a popular drag destination throughout the 1990s, although most serious clubbers would likely start the night there and end the night at La Cage. Lily White's Thursday Night Show, featuring first-time drag amateurs competing for high scores from audience judges, became an unusually comical tradition.

After the turn of the century, the neighborhood gentrified like wildfire, and long-abandoned properties were converted to residences. Now, people actually lived in the old Fifth Ward, which had been abandoned by everyone except gay bar owners since the 1940s. As quality of life improved, Club 219 plunged into a steep decline. Renovations were underway to modernize the bar in summer 2005, but the bar's future seemed deeply in doubt. Club 219 abruptly closed sometime in September 2005 without so much as a farewell show. Most furnishings were sold at auction in October 2005, and the property remained vacant for over fifteen years.

One month after Club 219's demise, La Cage owners George Prentice and Corey Grubb announced their retirement and relocation to Florida. New owners would run the landmark for the next twelve years.

Six months later, the M&M Club announced it would close after nearly thirty years in business. Founder Bob Schmidt, who had retired in 2002, returned for a week of family, community and nostalgia. Following a week of "lasts," including a final drag show, the M&M Club closed at bar time

Tiffany Thomas emcees in the early '90s. *B.J. Daniels.*

An all-star cast includes (*back row*) Sasha, Lily White, Shawna Love, (*front row*) Lena Chavez, Mary Richards, Baby Jane Hudson, Susan and Sage LaRue. *Lily White.*

on Sunday morning, May 13, 2006. In reflection, M&M Club received the loving send-off that Club 219 was denied.

CHANGING TIMES

While longtime customers were shocked by these significant changes, the younger generation didn't seem to notice. Something strange was already brewing in Milwaukee by 2007, and it wasn't the boom times that just brought seven new gay bars to town. Milwaukee had twenty-three gay bars—an unusual number for a city of its size—but the emerging generation didn't feel especially compelled to support them. Internet connectivity meant that LGBTQ people didn't need to go out to find love. Many bar-goers weren't seeking community anymore. They were seeking the best possible value and experience—and it didn't matter anymore if the bar was gay or straight. Hook-up sites had already created an alternative to meeting people in bars, and bar attendance would continue to decline over the next decade as apps became the dating norm.

Nobody would have imagined that only seven Milwaukee gay bars would survive to see the year 2020—or that 37 percent of all American gay bars would close in that same timeframe.

The warning signs were there. The *Milwaukee Journal Sentinel* revisited La Cage in February 2006, only to be shocked about the state of drag:

After hours of trying on wigs, painting on pouts, and squeezing silicone breast pads into dazzling dresses, Nova D'Vine, Jackie Roberts, Christina Chase and Shannon were ready to strut their stuff. The occasion: the weekly drag show at La Cage, a gay bar in Walker's Point. But first, the female impersonators had to deal with what's become a regular problem at La Cage and other gay clubs in the area: After all the work they put into getting ready, some people still weren't paying attention.

Club patrons at the bar stayed deep in conversation as performers took over the dance floor. Another group of "real" women in spaghetti-strap tanks and jeans bumped hips, danced and laughed—oblivious to the fact that they were dancing in the middle of a planned production.

"We get a lot of that. A lot of people get into the numbers, and they don't realize we're doing a show," said Shannon, who stayed in character and lip-synched Aretha Franklin while shooing the women out of the spotlight.

A scene like this probably wouldn't have happened in the mid-1980s and early '90s...but the fascination with female impersonators has cooled

Above: B.J. Daniels, Dominique Mahon and Duwanna Moore perform at Club 219. *B.J. Daniels.*

Left: Shawna Love backstage. *Shawna Love.*

in the past decade, some club owners say. The overexposure in the earlier era left up-and-coming performers with nowhere to go but down. Young people seemed less interested in drag shows and more focused on meeting people or dancing at clubs.

"The magic was in the air, honey, and it ain't there anymore," said Shawn Wandahsega, whose performance name is Shawna Love.

Top: Dita Von, Christina Chase and Shannon Dupree. *B.J. Daniels.*

Bottom: C'est La Vie star Jessica Daniels. *Jessica Daniels.*

The article goes on to explore the efforts of three gay bars (La Cage, C'est La Vie and Triangle, 135 East National Avenue) to bring drag back.

Interim La Cage owner Michael Jost planned to introduce Vegas-style female impersonator shows with steak and seafood dinners in a new $100,000 dinner theater.

New C'est La Vie owner Martin Belkin reopened the bar after founder John Clayton's death with plans to make it a friendly haven for all forms of gender expression. "I remember back when there was [Club] 219, I climbed over that fence [outside the bar] to see the show," said Misha Mahon, thirty-one, who was part of C'est La Vie's new cast. "I want there to be that enthusiasm again."

Triangle's owners planned to invest in traveling performers to keep a fresh, rotating show that audiences wouldn't find predictable, as well as three-dollar Long Island Iced Tea blends named after the performing girls.

None of these goals were ever really achieved. Although the Montage Show Lounge (now Jackie Roberts Show Lounge) did finally open in October 2009, high-dollar dinners were never on the menu. Triangle shifted its focus from drag to DJs until it closed in 2012. C'est La Vie is another story altogether.

C'EST LA VIE (1973–2008)

C'est La Vie was founded in 1973 and operated for thirty-three years by Clarence Germershausen, known as "John Clayton" to his friends and customers. The bar was the sixth to open in the emerging "gay village" but one of only three to survive the April 1974 conflagration. By 1976, it was an anchor of a new entertainment district that stretched from Oregon Street to St. Paul Avenue along Second and Water Streets, including Oregon House, Circus Disco, Ball Game, Leaded Shade, M&M Club, Wreck Room and the Factory. The 1976 GLIB Guide described C'est La Vie as "Mixed traffic. Pool table, dancing, loud talk. Busy bar block."

Although originally a men's bar, somewhat specializing as a pickup place for older men seeking younger guys, C'est La Vie began offering regular drag shows in the 1990s. The shows were not as competitive (or cutthroat) as those at La Cage or Club 219, but they certainly added creative energy the bar needed to survive. After Germershausen's death in September 2005, the bar struggled to stay viable in a rapidly changing neighborhood.

Entertainers, including Billie Blaze, Tabitha Stevens, Christina Chase, Tanya Michaels, Brittany Morgan, Joey Black, Jackie Roberts and Rudi D'Angelo. *William Hammerstad.*

C'est La Vie's closing was announced in April 2008. Showrunners planned a farewell show on Saturday, May 3, 2008, that would literally "bring down the house" on the last day of business. Incredibly, history nearly repeated itself. As the story goes, a queen who wasn't allowed to perform in the farewell show threatened to "blow up the bar" if she wasn't restored to the cast. Martin Belkin, already exhausted by three years of nonsense, shut down the show, the cast and the bar without any final hurrah. C'est La Vie, then the fourth-oldest gay bar in Wisconsin, just went dark forever.

Between 2006 and 2008, Milwaukee saw nine grand openings, including Kruz, which remains open today, but also extremely diverse venues like Club Tropical (626 South Fifth Street), Pumphouse (2011 South First Street) and Club Purr (3945 North Thirty-Fifth Street). These upstarts specialized in shows featuring African American and Hispanic queens, who were often the minority in other casts around Milwaukee. Despite ebb-and-flow crowds, all three venues were gone by 2010.

BRITTANY MORGAN

My first drag show was on Halloween 1980 at Sherlocks Home in Sheboygan. It was also the first time I went out dressed in public. The bar, then called Ye Olde Inn, had booked the Who's No Lady Revue from Milwaukee. I can't remember who opened the show, but I remember Ginger Spice, B.J. Daniels and Coco Lopez performing in the show. And I distinctly remember one song that stood out: "I Know What Boys Like" by the Waitresses, performed by Miss B.J. Daniels.

My very first performance was at Sam's in Madison in 1983. I was so bad that they wouldn't ask me back! Mable Kane was show director at the time. My roommate talked her into putting me into the show. She later told my roommate, "That little blonde doesn't belong on stage—don't ever ask me to put her in a show again!"

Ginger Spice was my biggest inspiration, in addition to Abby Rhodes, Holly Brown and B.J. Daniels. I tried to emulate them, but I was very shy and nervous, so they didn't welcome me into their circle right away. I moved to Milwaukee in 1985 and met Tina Capri while working at Pieces of Eight. She took me under her wing and introduced me to Mama Rae and Tiger Rose. They helped me a lot. Tiger made my first evening gown and taught me how to sew. Mama Rae and I would have long, deep talks about the community. She really guided me to the right people. Tina became my drag Mom. We would tear up the town some nights. She took me with her to all her shows.

Through Mama Rae, I knew drag had been going on for years and years before. When Ginger Spice was running Club 219, drag became even more popular across the city, state and entire Midwest. That really boosted the scene to new heights. The Baton Show Lounge was also very influential. When I started drag, all the Milwaukee girls wanted to emulate the Chicago girls. In time, the Milwaukee scene became just as competitive.

I started working at Miss Ms in 1987. Miss M put me on the map, so to speak. That's when I started doing more shows. Bobby from Jet's Place let me run a few shows, and so I became a regular. Bobby later bought Jet's Place with two other "Bs" and renamed it 3Bs. I continued to do shows there until 1996.

Believe it or not, I was the first drag queen John ever let into C'est La Vie. He never let me forget it. It was 1981. While I was walking from 219 to Phoenix, John stopped me and didn't believe I was a guy. He said, "Come here!" and led me into C'est La Vie, where he paraded me up and down the bar to see if anyone could tell I was a guy. It was too funny.

Brittany Morgan. *John Grant.*

Mandi Mc Call was the first showrunner at C'est La Vie from 1989 to 1994. It was traditionally a man's bar, but times were changing. John lost a lot of business during the AIDS crisis, and he thought it would help to have weekly shows and fundraisers. He was right—it really took off. The guys loved it! After Mandi was murdered in 1994, Tabitha Stevens took over the shows until she moved to Michigan in 1996. John asked me to be show director in 1996. I stayed ten years!

My favorite memory happened on New Year's Eve. I was on my second song on stage ("T'Amo") and suddenly the lights went out. All power was gone! The place was pitch black except for John's legendary flashlight. He always had that flashlight. Alvin was bartending. I think she gave away half the bar in the forty-five minutes the lights were off. It just so happened that there was an electrician in the bar. He went outside and discovered that someone had ripped the entire circuit breaker box off the back of the building. He fixed it by connecting it back together with a fork. Don't ask me how, but that's what John told me later.

Drag has really gone pretty far out since I stopped doing shows in 2006. The over-painting is what I'm talking about. It's become much stagier that it was between 1980 and 2010. Back then, we tried to look more real and glamorous. Now, it's all about painting for the back row, and that works for them now.

There were a lot of rumors about why C'est La Vie closed. Fact is, Marty didn't pay us one Saturday night, so we all quit. And by that time, it was too late to gain the business back. It was sad to see it close.

JACKIE ROBERTS (1972–2017)

Jackie Roberts came to La Cage in May 1989 and worked almost continuously until her departure in 2017. After spending twelve years as door girl, she was usually recognized as the front face of La Cage. When she retired, she performed a special three-hour going-away show and was presented with a

Jackie Roberts, Sasha, Christina Chase, Nova D'Vine and Billie Blaze. *William Hammerstad.*

formal sash and crown as the Official First Lady of La Cage. Jackie worked at La Cage longer than anyone, including Tony Aiello, who was resident DJ for almost twenty years.

"One Sunday night in 1989, I came here from Club Marilyn's underage night with some Milwaukee Ballet employees. I barely left the front bar, which was very dark at the time, and just stood against the wall taking it all in," Jackie said in 2009. "Two weeks later, I was back with some friends from Milwaukee High School of the Arts. After the shows, we talked with fans in the back bar (Jazz). We quickly learned it was all about working the door schedule and knowing when it was safe."

She became immediately fascinated by the star performers of that era: Holly Brown, Mimi Marks, Goldie Adams. Sunday night shows were at 10:30 p.m., and they were consistently packed. "At that time, you didn't see drag queens on TV. You couldn't watch a makeup tutorial on YouTube. There were no drag shows at brunches, dinners or street festivals. The scene

Jackie Roberts. *Howard Leu.*

was really deep underground," said Jackie. "You needed your drag mother to help you figure out this world."

Jackie and her best friend Rudy D'Angelo never missed a Sunday. They'd start the night with their high school friends at Club Marilyn and then sneak off to La Cage. One week, Jackie was pulled from the audience to work the spotlight for the show. "From there, I worked my way through every job in the bar—from the spotlight to cleaning to bar back to cast member to door girl to showgirl."

As much as things changed in twenty years, Jackie said she still worried about older, more isolated trans women finding each other in the world.

"People are always calling to see if it's ok to come in and walk around fully dressed as a woman. Some of these are older and more isolated girls who just want to know they'll be safe. Where would they go if we weren't here? Lots of people see this as just a club. They don't realize what being gay in Milwaukee would be like today if there hadn't been a La Cage."

Jackie could have written a book about what she saw and heard over the years. She remembered a lot of fistfights, a lot of wigs being pulled off and a whole lot of mayhem. She encountered many unique and unusual characters, including a Black queen from New York City who would command runway vogue competitions on the dance floor, or Miss Susan, a young lady who, oddly enough, dreamed of performing as a female illusionist.

"Lily White would paint her up and throw her on stage at 219 in lace gloves, crimped hair and pleather outfits. She would always try to get a show here, but never could. One night, we finally let her do a number. The audience was used to a more upscale performance, and they just didn't get it. Susan never performed here again. I wonder whatever happened to her."

Jackie fondly remembered Turnabout, where drag queens served drinks in their boy identities while the bartenders performed the drag show. ("It wasn't pretty!" she laughed.) She also remembered the strange combination of Taco Night with something called Dragstrip. Dragstrip involved drag queens stripping from girl to boy, pulling off fourteen layers of pantyhose, on top of the bar in heels, wigs scraping the ceiling.

"Drag in Milwaukee isn't what it used to be," Jackie said in 2009. "But it ain't dead. There aren't the sequins, beads or feathers you used to see. There aren't the faces, there aren't the voices. It's not as costumey, not as grand. Sometimes we'll see people performing in what they walked in wearing. You used to have to earn the right to be onstage. I always say, 'If you're not bleeding, sweating or crying, you are not trying hard enough!'"

After receiving a Lifetime Achievement Award in 2013, Jackie relocated to Kansas City for a short time. She returned to Milwaukee in 2015 and was soon diagnosed with cancer.

On January 5, 2017, Jackie Roberts left the stage forever. In September 2021, La Cage renamed its second-floor cabaret space the Jackie Roberts Show Lounge in her long-lasting memory.

DEAR RUTHIE

I believe I started in 1995. I'd been writing an advice column in the Wisconsin Light *newspaper. I had no intention of performing in drag; Ruthie was simply my pen name. However, the Madison Pride Parade organizers asked for Ruthie to appear in the parade, and the paper felt the publicity was too great to miss. I appeared as Ruthie in the parade, and we were amazed at the crowd response. Shortly afterwards, Karen Valentine*

Dear Ruthie in a fabulous costume. *Dear Ruthie.*

B.J. Daniels and Dear Ruthie.
John Grant.

invited me to perform in a show at the M&M Club. I loved every minute of it, and I've been writing and performing ever since.

This Is It was my hangout when I started drag. The gang there, particularly the bartender Ricky, always asked me to do my impersonation of actress Ruth Gordon. As a result, I quickly became known as Ruthie.

Drag reality competitions have forced performers to step up their games. Audiences expect so much more now, and rightly so. Back in the day, you performed in department store dresses or even hand-me-downs. There was no internet, making it hard to get wigs, gowns, etc. Now, it's so much easier to obtain the dazzling costumes and pieces that audiences expect. I'll also add that drag has grown and expanded into so many areas. Back in the day, the look was to capture the ideal femininity. The more a queen could "pass" as a cisgender woman, the better. Now, we have bearded queens—some of my favorite performers—as well as horror looks, and so much more. The entire "look" of drag has expanded so wonderfully.

I've had so much fun as Dear Ruthie. I was a reporter on a local late-night show, The Don & Bo Show, where they'd send me and a camera crew out to cover some unique, crazy, funny Milwaukee event. It was great fun, and the segments became the hit of the show. It was amazing seeing myself on billboards around the city. I almost got into a car accident once when a bus drove alongside me with my photo on the bus board.

Being a cohost on one of the country's few reality drag competitions was huge for me. Camp Wannakiki *becomes more popular across the nation every year. Being recognized by viewers around the country, touring California, appearing on podcasts…it's all wonderfully exciting. Shooting a reality show is tough work, but I look forward to filming every season, and I adore the friendships I've formed with every single contestant on the show.*

I think Milwaukee's LGBTQ community is very passionate. That passion, that drive, carries over into our drag scene. We're lucky to have such a varied, talented, large and wonderfully involved drag scene in our city.

NOVA D'VINE

Once upon a time, on a Sunday long ago, I walked into Club 219 and saw B.J. Daniels on stage.

I was mesmerized.

From that moment, I wanted to become a part of what that was. Drag was a bit more mysterious at that time. Glamour, illusion, beauty, the whole

Nova D'Vine and an epic Pride headdress. *Patrick Couillard.*

Nova D'Vine. *John Grant.*

cast was magical. It was a couple years later when fate made its call. In 1997, Joey Black brought me into the fold. The rest is history.

I feel blessed that I was embraced by the right people, and many stories later, I feel honored to have had my time in the spotlight. I feel proud to have created many memories and friendships along the way. The art of it will always be alive.

BRYANNA BANX$

It all started one Halloween playing dress up. And then, I started doing drag at OZ Nightclub in Wausau in 2004. That led to doing charity fundraiser shows for ARCW and other nonprofits.

In July 2005, I was convinced to enter my first drag pageant. I had no idea what was required, but I showed up, and I won against three other contestants! I was named the new Miss Gay Central Wisconsin USofA 2005.

I moved to Milwaukee in 2006, and I've performed at many spaces like Triangle, Monas, Fluid, C'est La Vie, M's, Art Bar, Viva La Femme, Club Purr, Tropical Nightclub, Hybrid Lounge, Hamburger Mary's, This Is It and D.I.X. I was awarded the title of Miss La Cage Nightclub in 2007 and became part of the Friday Night Transformations Show from 2010 to 2016.

Bryanna Banx$.
Bryanna Bank$.

In my opinion, Milwaukee has some of the best drag because of all the fabulous venues that allow us all to showcase and practice our talents. Giving us an outlet to be unique and perfect our craft any chance we wanted. Milwaukee is also home to some of the most well-known queens locally and nationally. They are continuously looking to pass down what they know and what they have learned. The newer generation is willing to accept the critique.

I have so many drag role models. I always point out those who helped me get to where I am at today by mentoring me and helping me every step of the way. Jackie Roberts, DuWanna Moore, Kelli Jo Klien, Shannon Dupree, Josie Lynn, Brandy Wells, Nova D'Vine, Kitanah Kim and Beja are just a few of my drag role models. I learned the art of drag the hard way by looking, listening and learning. I didn't have social media things like YouTube, Facebook, Instagram or even reality TV shows such as Ru Paul's Drag Race. *We had to learn the craft by trial and error. Doing pageantry really helped me zoom in on who I was and wanted to be, but also finding those drag sisters, aunties, uncles who were willing to help you and show you the path to success.*

JESSE RIVERA

The first drag show I ever attended was back in the '90s at Club 219. It was the premier bar for drag. Basically, it was "The Baton" of Wisconsin. Before becoming a show director, I was a promoter for the Miss Wi USofA system. The current Miss Wi USofA approached me and asked would I like to be a promoter and start my own prelim. I asked her, why me? She said, "I can see how much you love the art of drag." She told me that I would do a perfect job. I went ahead and started my prelim titled "Miss Gay City of Festivals USofA." I held that prelim for about fourteen years. In that time, I won several awards, including Best Prelim, Promoter of the Year and the Jimmy King award.

I became the show director at La Cage around 2013. Anastasia Devereaux was moving away, so the owners approached me. They said they loved how I ran my pageant prelim and that since I have good connections within the drag community, they thought I'd be a good fit as show director. Never had there been a show director who wasn't also a performer, but they said they believed in me and gave me a shot. I ran the shows successfully from 2013 until 2017, when George and Corey came back to the bar.

Left: Vanity Affair promotion. *Jesse Rivera.*

Right: Vanity Affair cast: Lady Gia, Chanel D'Vine, Jesse Rivera, Joey Jay, Jaida Essence Hall, Whitney Gaytan. *Jesse Rivera.*

I feel shows are successful in Milwaukee when there is diversity in the cast. By this, I mean I booked what I know people want. I'm not going to a dance club on a Saturday night, after having a long work week, just to hear a ballad. A high-energy cast is the key. Granted, not everyone is a dancer, but that's not what I meant. You must give the audience a little of everything: comedy, dance, glamour and, above all, professionalism. For the future of drag, I see drag taking a turn. By this, I mean it used to be all about who was the fishiest, and now it's more about the entertainment value of the performance. We shall see where the new generation of drag takes us!

TEMPEST HEAT

I started doing drag in 2007 when I met a queen named Misha Mahon. She was a trans drag queen who performed at C'est La Vie. She was the first person to put me in drag, and I fell in love with it immediately.

Anya Knees and Tempest Heat. *Tempest Heat.*

Before I met her, I would go to a Black gay bar in Riverwest called Emeralds. DJ Wayne would play all this Chicago house music, and all the kids would be vogueing in the bar. It was a small bar, but they still had drag shows. I fell in love seeing Shannon Dupree doing Patti LaBelle and Lady Symone doing Tina Turner. I loved Kenya Black, a gorgeous trans woman who was always half naked, but she had the body, so everyone loved watching her! I also saw Tracy Ross, another legendary performer, at Emeralds. And then there was Baja Bazaar. Oh, she was CAMP! I remember she came out in a gown made from Aldi grocery bags singing Erykah Badu's "Bag Lady." It was everything! Baja Bazaar, rest in peace.

Emeralds was the spot! But just down the street in Riverwest, there was a Black lesbian bar called Barbie Dolls Playhouse. The owner was a woman named Barbie. She was super nice and always had a live DJ playing Chicago house music as well. They sadly closed, but a new spot came along called Conversations. This was another gay bar, owned by an old friend of mine named Devon. I would go there every weekend, especially since I knew the owner well. There was also a Black gay bar in Walkers Point called Viva La Femme and a Black gay bar on Capitol Drive called Club Purr. Purr was owned by the people from Conversations, who closed that bar

Tempest Heat. *Tempest Heat.*

down so they could have the larger space. Purr was one of the first places I was ever a cast member. I performed on Thursday nights every week!

Thanks for including Black LGBTQ spaces. I think people forget about that aspect of Milwaukee gay history!

7

THE RISE OF THE RUGIRL (2009–)

Since the launch of *RuPaul's Drag Race* in 2009, Milwaukee drag has seen its greatest evolution yet. Just as the senior glamour queens of the 1960s and 1970s were replaced by the cinematic personalities of the 1980s, Milwaukee's 1990s drag stars found themselves eclipsed by millennial and Generation Y performers who were more colorful, more provocative, more defiant—and in some cases, more terrifying—than anything the city had ever seen before.

This new age of queens grew up in a world inspired by not only *Drag Race* and *Dragula* but also self-made drag celebrities on YouTube and Instagram who found virtual followings long before they found a paying gig. At the same time, this new generation was more accepting, more inclusive and more diverse than any generation before them. They challenged old-school rules excluding biological women and transgender women from drag. They applauded new forms of expression that leaned into horror, cartoon and fantasy. And they welcomed back crossover audiences, in numbers not seen since the golden age of drag, to sustain and celebrate their art.

Milwaukee became a springboard for international drag talent, sending no fewer than four performers to compete on *RuPaul's Drag Race* (Jaymes Mansfield, Trixie Mattel, Jaida Essence Hall and Joey Jay).

Male impersonation, in the form of "drag kings," fell out of favor in Milwaukee after vaudeville and was rarely, if ever, seen again. In 2004, Viktor Huge-O, Neil Down and Mario Belivadres Suave formed the Miltown Kings, devoted to the diversity of an all-inclusive and ever-changing community.

Indie film premiere at Hamburger Mary's with Veruca Voorhees, Dixie Kuppe, Trixie Mattel, Jaymes Mansfield, Vajay J Snappinturtle, Dear Ruthie and Dita Von. *B.J. Daniels.*

LEO LONG

The Miltown Kings were founded at the 2004 UWM Drag Ball. The founders saw no local representation for drag kings in Milwaukee. In fact, they were the only kings that had ever performed at the UWM Drag Ball. They were inspired by I.D.K.E (International Drag Kings Extravaganza), a yearly show and conference that attracts drag king troupes from all over.

> *I met the troupe at the Scorpio Party show. I'd seen pictures of kings in mags, but never seen one in person. Immediately, I was like I need to do that. I begged the troupe to let me be in the first show. I told them I would run crew or make flyers. Once I hit the stage for the first time, I fell in love and never left. I am still performing today almost twenty years later.*
>
> *We always considered ourselves more of a theater troupe than a bar troupe, although we did our share of bar shows, and this vastly affected how we put together acts or engaged with the audience. We specialize in large, choreographed group acts with five to fifteen performers, along with*

duets and solos. Our acts were often telling a short story in the length of a song. The shows ran the gamut of emotions, some funny or sexy. It was common for performers to do political acts, talk about social problems or express personal experiences through their acts. There was truly something for everyone at our show.

We created a family with our regular audience members. They were loyal. Not only did they come to every show in costumes, but they also put out our flyers, filled our crew rolls and helped so many other ways. We all kind of created a safe space together. We talked about consent, being gender nonconforming, polysexual relationships and kink relationships on stage before those were common conversations. We were a gathering place for folks who didn't feel like they fit in in the mainstream (queers, kinksters, thicc body people, furries, trans and nonbinary folks).

Our audiences were vastly diverse in almost every way possible. The Kings always reserved two acts every show for first-timers to try out. They would become part of the troupe for that show. We would invite them to practice for personal tutoring from troupe members. Several audience members got involved in drag or even became members through this opportunity. We often hosted drag workshops with the LGBT Center or at PrideFest, where people could learn how to do a drag transformation or even be transformed by our performers.

Drag king Colin Acumen performs at PrideFest Milwaukee. *Howard Leu.*

Miltown Kings cast on stage. *Miltown Kings.*

I would be remiss if I didn't mention what Miltown Kings did for the femme community. We had femme drag performers as full members since the beginning of our troupe. I really think having powerful independent femme representation like Ms. B Haven, Faye Tahl and Venus Envy—to mention just a few—really empowered the lesbian femme community in a beautiful and inspiring way. I had lots of audience members tell me over the years they loved Miltown Kings shows because they felt the most themselves there.

Drag taught me that, with hope and a lot of hard work, you can make magic. I was very shy and introverted, but those shows taught me to be fearless. It gave me a family that I still hold dear now. Drag taught me how to go out and get what I want. Drag taught me so much about myself and my gender. I have gone through many transformations over the years in that area and it has always given me a safe place to experiment and figure it out. Drag taught me to trust myself, be confident and, most importantly, to love the things that make me uniquely me.

Although the Miltown Kings dissolved in 2019, they left an indelible mark on the Milwaukee drag scene. Drag became more inclusive—of not only male impersonators but also biological women performing in character.

DIVINE TRASH

Annaleigh Vytlacil was just twelve years old when she first discovered Divine. After renting *Hairspray* from her local Hollywood Video, she became completely hooked on the character. As a natural performer, she joined the *Rocky Horror Picture Show* cast at the Oriental Theatre. While dressed as Babs Johnson from *Pink Flamingos* for a special movie villains drag show, she received overwhelming applause for her resemblance to Divine.

Over the past decade, Annaleigh brought Divine Trash: A Divine Impersonator to life at numerous venues throughout Wisconsin and Chicago. In 2016, she co-hosted the PrideFest Milwaukee Mainstage and performed at the Milwaukee LGBT Community Center's annual benefit. She's received high praise from the Divine estate and John Waters himself, who said Divine Trash is one of the best Divine impersonators he's ever seen.

While her star was rising, Divine Trash faced criticism, skepticism and even exclusion from a drag community not always welcoming to "bio queens" (aka biological females). She was told that her performances were not "real drag" and invalidated the art form.

"Some drag queens stick to the definition of 'dressed realistically as a girl,' and there is nothing wrong with that," said Divine Trash in 2017. "There's nothing wrong with that, but it doesn't need to be the rule. If you perform as a male character, you're a king. If you perform as a female character, you're a queen. And if you're performing with no gender, you are still royalty."

"Gender will forever be an issue with humans not willing to educate themselves," said Divine Trash. "One of the best ways to educate people is to platform more queer performers: drag kings, non-binary folx and, of course, females doing queen. The more we are seen and appreciated, the more respect and understanding we will receive. People tend to think they're the authority on what drag is, when in truth, none of us are truly the authority. Respect people. Respect their art. It's as simple as that."

Divine Trash, outrageous Divine impersonator. *Annaleigh Vylactil.*

BRANDON AND ASHLEY WRIGHT

Sharing the Hamburger Mary's dressing room: Shea Coulee, Kim Chi and Trixie Mattel. *Brandon and Ashley Wright.*

Hamburger Mary's originally opened in 1972 in the SoMa District of San Francisco. It was an eclectic burger joint, where everyone was welcome. One of their early slogans was "an open-air bar & grill for open-minded people." From those humble beginnings, Hamburger Mary's has grown into an international franchise system, with locations across America and Mexico.

In 2007, ownership of the Hamburger Mary's brand changed hands to its current owners (Brandon and Ashley Wright, then owners of the Chicago location, and Dale Warner, then owner of the West Hollywood location). "We were not only the owners and operators of a Hamburger Mary's location, but also co-owners of the master franchise, Hamburger Mary's International (HMI). While living in Chicago, we visited Milwaukee often and always loved the city. It only made sense that our second location would be in the Cream City. Now, we both call Milwaukee home!" said Wright.

> *Hamburger Mary's has helped bring drag into the mainstream. Even though Hamburger Mary's is an LGBTQ establishment, many of our customers are not part of the LGBTQ community. For many, it is their first encounter with drag performers, or even their first encounter with LGBTQ people. Being an all-ages restaurant, as opposed to a twenty-one-plus nightclub or bar, Hamburger Mary's truly makes drag accessible to everyone.*

TRIXIE MATTEL

The first time Brian Firkus saw a drag queen, he was eighteen years old and doing the *Rocky Horror Picture Show* at Milwaukee's Oriental Theater. "I thought this cast member was just so beautiful," he said. "One night, she skipped a show, and I had to fill in for her. Just think, if she hadn't missed that show, I might never have done drag."

Trixie Mattel performing at PrideFest. *Howard Leu.*

Fast forward twelve years, and Trixie Mattel was named fourth among "the most powerful drag queens in America" by *New York* magazine. Her sixth-place run on season 7 of *RuPaul's Drag Race* made history: she was the first queen to return for a multi-episode run following elimination. Next, she headlined *RuPaul's Drag Race All-Stars* (2018) as the first-place winner of season 3. The breakout queen, already famous for her comedy tours, web series, podcasts, record albums and published works, launched a cosmetics empire in 2019 and an ambitious Palm Springs motel project in 2021. She was immortalized as an actual, collectible doll by Mattel and Integrity Toys. With two new reality series on the way, Mattel began 2022 with a new single, "This Town," and the announcement of her fourth studio album.

Yet when Trixie Mattel burst on the Milwaukee scene, traditional drag fans were completely confused. "I had the skin of a Barbie, the proportion of a Polly Pocket and the hair of My Little Pony," said Trixie. "I had so many inspirations: Barbie, Divine, Dolly Parton, Audrey from *Little Shop of Horrors*, Jessica Rabbit, Peg Bundy....People did not know what to make of me. I wasn't your typical pageant queen, that's for sure."

Trixie did a weekly event at La Cage for two years, as well as a weekly bingo show at Hamburger Mary's. In 2015, she headlined Trixie's Funhouse at PrideFest Milwaukee. After performing in Chicago, she realized there was a wide world of opportunity ahead.

Chicago celebrated its drag queens for who they are and what they're good at, rather than comparing them to what drag was perceived to be. My look became more severe, my comedy became darker, and people had a genuine response. When you pulled the string on my back, I didn't say, "Let's go shopping," I made a sinister joke about depression. People didn't expect to hear that, but it resonated with them.

You'd be amazed, me being a drag queen, and doing guitar, and tap dancing, and working with puppets, people think I'm from another planet, because the bar has been set so low for drag queens. Nowadays, someone can just get dressed up and become famous on Instagram.

Drag is such a subversive art form that you can do truly anything with. Drag was born in gay clubs at 1:00 a.m. on a Monday. I don't understand how in an art form where people can do whatever they want people can ask "Trixie Mattel, why do you paint so differently?"' I'm like, why would everyone paint the same? That's the more pressing question. Are you really an artist if you're just emulating every drag queen that came before you?

Trixie and Kim Chi perform in Milwaukee. *Patrick Farabaugh.*

> *It's important to me to make a mark. I had a need to make a mark in the arts community. I know someday after I die, people will be able to reference my look and say, "That's so Trixie Mattel," and that's important to me. All my favorite drag queens—Jackie Beat, Lady Bunny, Coco Peru—all had a very strong visual. A strong visual is what makes you memorable and makes people remember you. You'll always remember my name and what I looked like.*

"Drag is subversive at its core, it's always going to be against the grain," said Trixie. "If you want to see drag queens put on sensible dresses and say nice things about each other, well, I don't want to go to that show. Do you?"

Trixie had her first alcoholic beverage—a Tootsie Roll—at This Is It in 2010. When she was cast on *Drag Race*, owners installed TVs behind the bar so she could host viewing parties. In 2021, she became part owner of the historic bar and is now guiding an inclusive, colorful and exciting future.

"I'm still a businessperson," said Trixie, "and I still believe that this business is the Cher of gay bars. You know, it'll be looking the same in another fifty years."

DITA VON

I was first introduced to the art of drag at age fifteen or sixteen. I was in a production of Anything Goes *with the Peter Quince Performing Company in Manitowoc. My good friend Tyler Wicihowski, aka Ellen Diamond, and I shared a dressing room that summer. Halfway through the show during intermission break, Tyler would apply his drag makeup and wear large sunglasses for the second half of the show. After the curtain went down at the Capitol Civic Centre for* Anything Goes, *Tyler would hop into his Cadillac and drive south to Milwaukee to perform at Club 219. I was mesmerized by the power of makeup and transformation! I thought, "If I ever move to Milwaukee, I'm going to do drag too!" And here we are!*

Tyler/Ellen Diamond was my first OG drag mother. She would do my makeup as I listened with full attention to her stories about shows and drag in Milwaukee. I remember watching RuPaul on VH1 in her original series and being star struck by her beauty, glamour and transformation. When the internet came around and I discovered YouTube, that opened a whole new door to see other drag queens and their performances. Lypsinka always stood out to me! Her performances were captivating.

After moving to Milwaukee, I had two drag mothers (Anastasia Deveraux and Betty Boop) who mentored me, supported me and helped me gain traction on becoming Dita Von. I started performing in Milwaukee around 2012, after a few years of doing amateur appearances at Manitowoc fundraisers such as Relay for Life (American Cancer Society) and Heart-A-Rama (American Heart Association). As a new girl, I was grateful to find a sisterhood of kindness, support and love. B.J. Daniels, Nova D'Vine, Jackie Roberts and Karen Valentine treated me as a sister, not competition. I could never thank them enough.

I would say my drag is a little on the old-school side. My aesthetic has been influenced heavily by my love for the glamour of "Old Hollywood." In my performance style, I'm definitely all about the sparkle, the stage presence and telling a story through delivering my performance.

My favorite drag career moment was performing at halftime for the Milwaukee Bucks Pride Night Game at Fiserv Forum! The venue is beautiful, and the experience was unforgettable.

RuPaul's Drag Race has lifted the art of drag outside of the LGBTQ+ community. Allies, supporters and even those girls' night out and bachelorette party crowds have helped factor into an increase in attendance at shows.

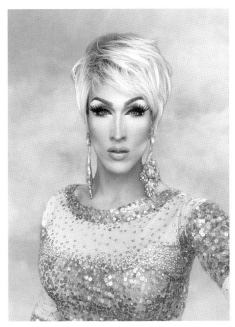 

Left: Dita Von, TikTok sensation. *Dita Von.*

Right: Dita Von performing at PrideFest. *Howard Leu.*

Unique performances at D.I.X. Milwaukee. *Meg Strobel.*

Drag is a celebration of our differences in an experience that brings us together. Milwaukee has always been such a diverse city, and we embrace that diversity in the drag experience. It is exhilarating to watch new performers expressing themselves as their best selves. The creativity, the innovation, the drive to try new and daring things: that's what keeps drag exciting in Milwaukee. The unexpected always keeps people coming.

JAIDA ESSENCE HALL

Jaida had been performing drag for nine years when she was cast on the twelfth season of *RuPaul's Drag Race*. In 2010, she entered a drag competition for $500, but the competition collapsed when her competitors dropped out.

As a former Miss Five, Miss Gay Madison, Miss Wisconsin Club and Miss City of the Lakes, Jaida emerged victorious as the winner of *RuPaul's Drag Race* season 12. She has toured nearly nonstop ever since with Drive'N Drag, Night of the Living Drag, A Drag Queen Christmas and other events. She was recently added to the cast of RuPaul's Drag Race Live! in Las Vegas.

"A lot of times, I reflect on where I came from and what should have been a possibility for me, and now through drag, all of this has changed," Hall told the *Milwaukee Journal Sentinel* in 2020. "Sometimes, I feel like it's a dream."

"Doing the halftime show at the Milwaukee Bucks game was a highlight of my career," said Hall. "Everyone was cheering my name, in Milwaukee's biggest arena, and the applause went on forever. I've never felt so supported. Without the people here in Milwaukee first loving and supporting me, I would not be who I am today. I would not have the confidence that I have in drag."

Hall credits her grandmother—a "super glamorous woman"—for accepting him for who he was, even when he didn't know himself.

"I'm thankful I had a family who understood that I was different," Hall told *Attitude* magazine in 2020, "but never made me feel bad about it. That gave me the confidence to be who I am."

"When I came back to performing in 2012, many new queens had emerged on the scene during my break from the stage," said B.J. Daniels. "Jaida Essence Hall immediately stood out to me as both a beautiful and talented queen. I was fortunate enough to be able to work with her, as well

Top: Jaida Essence Hall. *Patrick Farabaugh.*

Middle: B.J. Daniels and Jaida at PrideFest 2019. *Mike Hiller.*

Right: D.I.X. cast of characters. *Meg Strobel.*

as watch her grow into a well-rounded performer and emcee as a fan. She brought the house down at my annual PrideFest show in 2019."

"The drag scene in Milwaukee is so diverse," Jaida told *Milwaukee* magazine in 2020. "You can go out on any given night and see anything. It's not just one thing…it's an eclectic mix of so many different things we've learned from each other over time."

"I might not be what a lot of people expect or want me to be, but I'm loving all of it regardless," said Hall. "It feels good to be representing my city…it's a way to give back to the city…and it's given a lot of people here hope that they can do whatever they want."

MELEE McQUEEN

I began drag because I see it as a transformative art form. The ability to become a different creative variation of yourself on a whim is like magic. Drag lets me live out the superstar fantasy using all the creative skills including design, theater, music and photography. It's a privilege when you can do what you love and get paid for it. My parents are immigrants from Vietnam. They've had to hustle the majority of their lives to allow me to even think about dressing up as a job. So, drag for me stays a passion with high standards because my parents didn't have the illusion of reality TV success and luxury of fantasy.

MALAIYA MARVEL

I got my first taste of drag as a coordinator for the UW–Whitewater Drag Show. I was deeply inspired by local legends Tempest Heat and Jaida Essence Hall. I made my first drag appearance in 2014. Since then, Malaiya has evolved into a cosplay drag queen with roots in nerd culture. I feel I'm inspiring a new generation of nerdy entertainers to be themselves through creative artistic expression. Milwaukee's alternative drag scene welcomes exploration.

JASON LUU/MELEE

Model / Entertainer / Influencer

Above: Chameleon Melee McQueen exemplifies the multitasking queen. *Melee McQueen*.

Left: Malaiya Marvel, cosplay queen. *Malaiya Marvel*.

JOEY JAY

Joey Jay, sensational dancer and performer. *Joey Jay.*

I grew up in Madison, Wisconsin, and came to Milwaukee in 2011 to pursue a career in ballroom dance. I taught every day and competed on the weekends, but it wasn't filling the creative void as well as I had hoped. I would do my students' makeup for competitions, choreograph their routines and constantly try to convince them to do routines to Britney, Beyonce, Ariana or any other pop diva I was obsessed with. I was living vicariously through my students.

I watched RuPaul's Drag Race *religiously for years. I was always enthralled by the queens. I had snuck into a few national pageants, seeing Alyssa Edwards, Aurora Sexton, Candi Stratton, India Ferrah, all for the first time. They were all superstars to me. I was lucky enough to start conversations and stay in touch through the years. When I decided to put my name into the drag Goblet of Fire, I picked all of their brains. I still keep in touch with all of them and consider them huge influences on my drag career.*

In fall 2016, I called Dita Von and asked her to come over and paint my face. I was unhappy in my job and feeling stuck in my life. The next day, she arrived at my apartment—aka the "Lake Drive Drag Academy," where Trixie Mattel lived before me—and beat my face with all the colors she liked to use. I remember FaceTiming one of my makeup artist friends to share the final results. I was so inspired! The next morning, I went to the nearby theater store and bought every product Dita recommended.

I practiced every day. By November, I felt confident enough to step out in public and book a few shows. My roommate, Reid LePage, produced a party called SWELL: An Upscale Party on the Downlow, where I made my drag debut. The following week, Jesse Rivera booked me as a guest at La Cage's Saturday night show. I had the opportunity to dance for Coco Montrese at PrideFest Milwaukee 2016.

I've never liked to conform. My drag is the lipstick lesbian you never asked for: sexy, tomboy….I joke I am more masculine in drag than out of. I've never been a huge fan of the wig look. I love using my own hair. I've heard critique after critique that I need to edit my look, how I won't get booked in shows if I don't switch it up. I played the game for awhile, but always snuck in a number without a wig. I'd already been submitting content to RuPaul's Drag Race *to prepare myself for the inevitable question from the judges' panel: "but where's your wig?"*

Drag was already becoming mainstream when I started, after season after season of Drag Race *on TV, but it's even more mainstream now. Today, kids have so much more exposure, are starting earlier, are following the judges' critiques and are polished enough by eighteen (or even younger) to get booked in local shows. It's only going to become more mainstream. It's the modern punk era. We now have drag queens accepting awards, walking red carpets, touring the world as superstars. It's only going to keep getting bigger and better.*

A few years ago, I moved to Phoenix and started my life in a new city. But I love coming back home to my home state. Over the past several months, I was able to book shows in Madison and Milwaukee. My mother lives in Madison, so I take any chance I have to visit her. She is my number-one supporter. I love seeing all the new faces popping up on social media, watching them win amateur contests and host their own nights at my old venues. The scene is incredibly welcoming whenever I come back.

Drag is progressing so quickly. When I started going out, drag was just about the clubs. Today, we have queens running for office, putting out music, acting onstage, appearing in major motion pictures. I love seeing this for our community. When you get into the gig, you are a walking political statement which the world needs to see. There is still so much work ahead of us. For example, the "Don't Say Gay" bill in Florida. But we will persevere and overcome. And we will inspire young kids to live their lives as their authentic selves.

ABIGAIL BEVERLY HILLZ

I chose to participate in the art form of drag because it inspires me to be more creative and open as a person. As a drag entertainer, I love to design and sew my costumes, style the hair that I wear and come up with conceptual performances. I happen to run the only entirely trans casted regular drag show in Wisconsin called Do You Worship the Dolls? *at* This Is It bar.

Being a woman—who is also trans outside of drag—pushes me to love and celebrate my body even more through the sensuality that comes

Abigail Beverly Hillz is a fast-rising star on the Milwaukee scene and demands inclusive drag for women. *David Martinez.*

with drag entertainment. However, it has presented challenges with other entertainers who may not approve of me being a woman in a queen's space. Many drag queens are cisgender gay men.

However, I don't let that bother me. I define my drag—and no one can take that from me! I see Milwaukee's drag scene continuing to diversify and grow and become more accepting. Milwaukee is full of incredibly talented queens and kings. And I'm excited beyond belief to see more trans entertainers grace the stages soon!

GEORGE SCHNEIDER

As Wisconsin's longest-running gay bar, This Is It crackles with a vibrant newness that continues to surprise and delight its customers. In 2018, the bar celebrated its fiftieth anniversary with ambitious expansion plans that doubled its floor plan; added a cabaret space, dance floor and second bar; and increased the venue's capabilities to achieve a much larger vision. Although This Is It hosted occasional drag shows over the years, the bar really wasn't known for it. That all changed in 2019, when the doors opened to the expanded space. While pandemic restrictions closed most bars and canceled pride festivals, This Is It hosted virtual events throughout 2020 and 2021, including entirely digital Pride Weekends with high-profile headliners.

This Is It offers Milwaukee's most diverse drag talent. *George Schneider.*

In an era where popular opinion was that "gay bars are dead, social media has made them irrelevant," I begged to differ. I saw the main reason that many longtime queer spaces were closing as a direct result of a refusal to change and adapt. The drag scene is and always has been an anchor of queer nightlife. In the advent of shows like RuPaul's Drag Race, *the popularity of drag has soared. It was only advantageous that we adapted to the times. We wrapped our arms around our performers and provided not only a space for them to perform but also a formula for the bar to endure well beyond its fiftieth anniversary.*

In the past, most of our shows were pop-ups and infrequent in nature. When Trixie Mattel (now co-owner) started her run on Drag Race, *we started taking steps to offer more frequent shows, including many national names from* RuPaul's Drag Race.

Since 2019, This Is It has offered a performance space for emerging artists aged eighteen to twenty-one. *George Schneider.*

Before the expansion, we would lose money when we brought the big names in! Not too many people know this. The space was so small, and the booking fees were so high, that it was nearly impossible to make a profit. We were happy to break even, albeit rare in these instances. I viewed it as a "marketing investment" knowing that my late business partner Joe and I were dreaming and scheming even back then about expansion.

Trixie and I had been talking partnership for some time. When we were considering expansion, she first reached out to me, but the timing just wasn't right because of her cosmetics launch. I know the narrative exists out there that Trixie swooped in with a big bag of money to save us from COVID, but that's not the case. We survived and emerged strong because of our ability to adapt with the help of our community.

It is true, however, that her name brings us out of the COVID scenario in a much more powerful way. When someone has the international recognition and notoriety like she does, it can only benefit any venture she's attached to. This was part of our mutual calculus for the partnership from the get-go. We both love the bar and our hometown, so we want it to

Marbella Sodi leads the way for Milwaukee's Latinx performing community. *Patrick Farabaugh.*

thrive. If there is one thing the partnership has affected where shows are concerned, it's the clout factor of performing at "Trixie's Bar." Instead of us reaching out to the big names, they now reach out to us. Trixie and I love this, but our first commitment and priority is to our local and regional performers first!

What's the future of drag in Milwaukee? Three words: inclusion, diversity and variety. The drag venues that will do well and thrive will embody those three elements. I also think that the performers' pay will be a factor for a successful venue. Pay that is fair, consistent and considers the amount of work that goes into performing.

CALLING DOWN THE SPIRITS

Since 2021, This Is It has also become the home of MKE Vogue Nights, a ballroom house competition sponsored by the Empowering Community

Left: Model Dickie Knox at Vogue Nights working the runway. *Glenda Wallace.*

Right: Young attendees at Vogue Nights demonstrate energetic and diverse new talent. *Glenda Wallace.*

Action Initiative, a grass-roots organization led by queer people of color (QPOC) and Health Connections Inc.

The monthly series, happening every third Wednesday at This Is It, is planned by community leaders Ricardo Wynn (aka Tee Tee Mizrahi) and Chad Carroll, representing the Milwaukee chapters of the Iconic International House of Mizrahi (founded in 1992 in Brooklyn) and the House of Dimera Alain-Mikli. Monthly themes and categories are heavily anticipated—and eagerly announced on social media two to three weeks in advance—so contestants can get their look on.

Every month, 250-plus people come together in downtown Milwaukee as a true community: celebrating a shared history and heritage, competing in extravagant exhibitions, cultivating new friendships and families, connecting to critically important health resources, enjoying a shared meal and collaborating on a stronger, healthier, more vibrant future for all.

But MKE Vogue Nights are much, much more than just a ballroom competition. The program strives to bridge healthcare and racial disparities, while creating a haven for QPOC/LGBTQ self-expression. In addition to celebrating a creative subculture, the Nights deliver a wide array of health and wellness resources.

"I don't know a space where you can go to get a feeling of belonging, a feeling you can be somebody, a chance to create or re-create yourself, as well as food, drink, entertainment and healthcare," said Ricardo Wynn. "Vogue Nights show how much we can achieve as a collective community."

Seven generations after sordid stories of William Dorsey Swann scandalized small-town Milwaukee, his spiritual descendants have brought ballroom house and queer community back to the streets, inspiring the next generation of Milwaukee drag to be more vibrant, diverse and outrageous than ever before.

CURTAIN CALL

We acknowledge that this history may have some omissions, simply because of the wide, deep and lasting legacy of Milwaukee drag and the path that these proud pioneers carved into our landscape so that others could thrive.

When all is said and done here, the end purpose of this work is to expand the ideas of drag not only as theatrical expressions of gender and social commentary but also as a beacon of "otherness" that has and will always continue to attract participants to its show biz tent. It may also be seen as a family tree that keeps expanding exponentially worldwide, adding more nuance to what can only be described as a uniquely LGBTQ art form, one that is open to all who want to shed oppression, spread their glittery wings and fly in the face of convention.

After seven generations, we are merely at an intermission—a moment in time between what has gone before and what's about to happen—and the future is brighter than ever. So, please, take your seats. The curtain is about to rise for an all-new cast—and you won't want to miss a moment.

And the show goes on!

Spreading joy in the streets of Walker's Point. *Cormac Kehoe.*

ABOUT THE AUTHORS

B.J. DANIELS was always dreaming big. Through many a turn of events, those dreams came true in ever so many ways. Always looking for outlets to use their talent for art, theater and costuming became the backbone of what would become a life jam-packed with those very things. In other words, doing drag led to hair and makeup work on set for film and video, which led to teaching and learning the art of hairdressing as a licensed professional, which led to assignments in fashion for regional magazines, which led to covering Fashion Week in NYC for many years. B.J. still works behind the chair and lens and still performs in drag here and there as time and energy allow. Being an older queen ain't for sissies, that's for sure. Documenting history of the LGBT community has become another passion for them, and who knows what the future will hold?

MICHAIL TAKACH is a historian, author, reporter and communications professional living in Los Angeles. He earned his master's degree in communications and history at the University of Wisconsin. As a sixth-generation Milwaukeean, Michail has always been fascinated by local facts, fictions and folklore. He has supported various nonprofit organizations over the past two decades, including Milwaukee Pride, where he was communications director for ten years. As the curator of the Wisconsin LGBTQ History Project, Michail produces ongoing articles, documentaries and podcasts about local history. Although his career has taken him to the West Coast, Michail will always have deep roots in Milwaukee.

Visit us at
www.historypress.com